Strength to Be Holy

Don Thorsen, Editor

EMETH PRESS
www.emethpress.com

Strength to Be Holy

Copyright © 2014 Don Thorsen
Printed in the United States of America on acid-free paper

All rights reserved. No part of this book may be reproduced, or stored in a retrieval system or transmitted in any form or by any means, electronic, mechanical, photocopying, recording, scanning or otherwise, except as permitted by the 1976 United States Copyright Act, or with the prior written permission of Emeth Press. Requests for permission should be addressed to: Emeth Press, P. O. Box 23961, Lexington, KY 40523-3961. http://www.emethpress.com.

Library of Congress Cataloging-in-Publication Data

Strength to be holy / edited by Don Thorsen.
  pages cm
 ISBN 978-1-60947-073-9 (alk. paper)
 1. Holiness--Christianity--Sermons. 2. Wesleyan Church--Sermons. 3. Sermons, American--20th century. 4. Sermons, American--21st century. 5. Azusa Pacific University. I. Thorsen, Donald A. D., editor of compilation.
 BT767.S77 2014
 234'.8--dc23
                         2013047926

Front cover
Photo of the Cross Towers at Azusa Pacific University taken by David Johnson

Dedication

To the
Azusa Pacific University
Graduate School of Theology
Students, Faculty, Administration, and Staff

Contents

Acknowledgements / ix

Introduction: Holiness—God's Calling for Christians
    Don Thorsen / 1

Part 1: Nature of Holiness

1. Holiness Is What We Long For
   Don Thorsen / 9
2. The Holy River of God
   Kevin W. Mannoia / 19
3. The Aroma of Holiness
   Lynn Allan Losie / 25

Part 2: Our Holy God

4. The Holy God of Compassionate Power
   Tony Baron / 33
5. The Philippian Hymn: Ode to the Servant
   Russell Duke / 45
6. The Trinitarian Life of Faith
   Brian Lugioyo / 55

Part 3: Hope of Holiness

7. Living the Reality of Death and Resurrection
   Kent Walkemeyer / 63

8. Esther's Banquet of Hope
   Karen Strand Winslow / 73
9. Who am I? Recovering Biblical Identity
   Linda Pyun / 83

Part 4: Pursuit of Holiness

10. On Becoming a Pearl Merchant and Learning to Please God
    Roger White / 95
11. A Lesson from the Kernel
    Daniel Newman / 105
12. It's Not Too Late to Be Holy
    Sarah Sumner / 113

Part 5: Holy Practices

13. Holiness Takes Practice
    T. Scott Daniels / 125
14. Sanctify Them in the Truth; Your Word Is Truth
    Timothy Finlay / 135
15. Spiritual Formation in an Age of YOLO: 'You Only Live Once'
    Keith Matthews / 143
16. Prayer: God's Power-Sharing Device
    Gary Black, Jr. / 149

Part 6: Social Holiness

17. Loving My Neighbor
    Deborah Hearn-Chung Gin / 161
18. Inspirational Sayings
    Rob Muthiah / 171
19. Violence and Passivity vs. Jesus' Third Way
    Paul Alexander / 181

Epilogue: No Holiness but Social Holiness
    Don Thorsen / 189

Appendices
    Appendix 1: The Holiness Manifesto / 193
    Appendix 2: Fresh Eyes on Holiness: Living Out the Holiness Manifesto / 197

List of Contributors / 201

Acknowledgements

I want to acknowledge people who helped me in the completion of *Strength to Be Holy*. To begin, I thank Larry Wood for his work as my publisher with Emeth Press. Larry has long served as a mentor and friend of mine as well as publisher.

Next I thank Carmeli Silva for her expertise and enthusiasm in promoting ministry in general and ministry training in particular in the Azusa Pacific Graduate School of Theology. Dean Scott Daniels was supportive of this book project in honor of the 30th Anniversary of the Graduate School of Theology, and Steve Wilkens continues to be a friend and encourager of Christian scholarship. Kevin Mannoia also gave me helpful advice in framing this book.

Most importantly I thank my colleagues in the Graduate School of Theology, especially those who contributed sermons to this book. Alfred Lord Tennyson said, "I am a part of all that I have met." This statement certainly applies to me because I have been enriched by those with whom I have worked at Azusa Pacific University. I have benefited from the minds and spirit of many people in the Graduate School, especially faculty dedicated to the training of men and women for clergy and lay positions of leadership in churches. It is my hope that I have contributed as much to others as I have received during my years of service in the University.

Finally, I thank my daughters—Liesl, Heidi, and Dana—for their constant affirmation and encouragement. Their love helps to sustain my calling as a professor, preacher, and author as well as father.

Introduction

Holiness—God's Calling for Christians

Don Thorsen

Holiness represents both an ancient and enduring theme of biblical Christianity. Although some consider the term to be old-fashioned or impractical, the authors of this volume consider holiness to be at the heart of their understanding of God and of God's calling for Christians to be holy. As it says in 1 Peter 1:15-16, "Instead, as he [God] who called you is holy, *be holy* yourselves in all your conduct; for it is written, 'You shall *be holy*, for I am holy'" (NRSV, emphasis mine). This biblical exhortation is not considered merely symbolic, or an unachievable goal to which no Christian may believably reach. Instead holy living is the lifestyle to which God calls Christians, not because God expects them to achieve Christlikeness on their own human power or merit, but because of God's grace.

As Christians, we have received the gift of salvation by grace through faith because of the life, death, and resurrection of Jesus Christ, our Savior. Just as Jesus desires to become our Savior, he also desires to become the Lord of our lives. Already Jesus is the Lord of the universe, but he may not yet be the Lord of all our beliefs, values, and practices.

Jesus' lordship in people's lives ordinarily occurs subsequent to their respective conversion. Only after growth in God's grace and in responsible obedience to that grace may Christians hope to love God with their whole heart, soul, mind, and strength, and to love their neighbors as themselves (see Mark 12:18-31).

By consecrating their lives to God, through various means of grace and spiritual disciplines, God's Holy Spirit provides Christians the strength to be holy—the gracious ability to fulfill the commands of God in Scripture and to receive the fullness of God's promised blessings available in our present lives. We look forward to the complete fulfillment of our salvation in heaven, but in the time being God wants us to live lives characterized by holiness, love, justice, forgiveness, and other Christian virtues in this world: spiritually and physically, individually and communally, ministerially and socially.

Sermons on Biblical Holiness

This volume contains a selection of sermons written by members of the Graduate School of Theology at Azusa Pacific University. The sermons were compiled in honor of the Thirtieth Anniversary of the Graduate School. Contributors include past and present educators, who have served full-time as faculty and administrators. They worked expertly and sacrificially in the preparation of students for positions of clergy and lay leadership in churches and other Christian organizations. Their sermons give insight into who they are as leaders—as Christians dedicated to the ministry of the gospel of Jesus Christ—and to what they have taught in the Graduate School.

The topic of holiness is apropos for the Graduate School of Theology, and also for the University at large. Azusa Pacific's Position Statement on Evangelical Commitment states its historic theological foundations: "Reflecting our Wesleyan-Holiness heritage, we consider right living important along with right belief. We seek truth primarily through Scripture and integrate other sources such as reason, tradition, and experience." As such, both the Wesleyan and Holiness traditions of Christianity are indispensable to the theological undergirding of the University. In fact, the emphasis on holiness served as the theological glue, so to speak, that united the Quakers and Methodists who founded the institution in 1899 as a Training School for Christian Workers.

Of course, it is no easy task to maintain the theological heritage of any Christian institution of higher education, and Azusa Pacific is no exception. For example, James Tunstead Burtchaell wrote a book entitled *The Dying of the Light: The Disengagement of Colleges and Universities from their Christian Churches* (1998), and he described Azusa Pacific University as one of two evangelical institutions becoming disengaged from their theological heritage. Although Azusa Pacific has never been formally affiliated with a specific Christian church or denomination, its holiness background united many of the individuals, churches, and denominations that support the University. Thus, it is hoped that this volume will help to highlight and promote the holiness heritage of both Azusa Pacific and the Graduate School of Theology, lest one of the most crucial theological foundations of the institution be lost.

What Is Holiness?

This book is not a biblical or theological treatise on the nature of holiness. It is more sermonic than apologetic. Yet we are sympathetic toward those for whom the themes of holiness, spiritual formation, and Christian discipleship are not commonplace. For those interested in learning more about biblical holiness, I recommend reading the two appendices in this volume.

The first appendix consists of "The Holiness Manifesto," which summarizes the message of biblical holiness for the twenty-first century. It represents a convergence document written by participants in the Wesleyan Holiness Study Project, held at Azusa Pacific University. The Wesleyan Holiness Study Project was instituted by Kevin Mannoia, who is a contributor to this volume, and it drew upon insights from dozens of scholars, pastors, and church leaders from various Wesleyan, Methodist, Holiness, and Pentecostal denominations. The "Holiness Manifesto" was published by Eerdmans in a book by the same name in 2008. It represents a brief statement about the message of biblical holiness, its relevance for people today—individually and socially, spiritually and physically—and how Christians ought to promote biblical holiness.

The second appendix contains "Fresh Eyes on Holiness: Living Out the Holiness Manifesto." It is a brief document that helps local pastors (and churches) consider major issues, which must be engaged, as pastors look to the future in leading their congregations in deeper embodiment of the holiness message. "Fresh Eyes on Holiness" was also written by participants of the Wesleyan Holiness Project. The document was intended to be a practical aid in applying principles of biblical holiness for Christians and churches today, and also for impacting society as a whole, including care for God's creation.

Strength to Be Holy

It is difficult to choose a title for a volume of sermons on the topic of holiness, which includes writings about faith development, spiritual formation, and Christian discipleship. My choice of a book title reflects the influence of another anthology of sermons written by Martin Luther King, Jr., entitled *Strength to Love*. King's sermons powerfully talk about his Christian calling to spread the biblical message of love—holistically conceived—especially through the Civil Rights Movement in the United States during the 1950-60s. It should be obvious that his book title inspired the title of this book.

In a similar way, we in the Graduate School of Theology are called to spread the biblical message of holiness—holistically conceived—through our preaching, teaching, leadership, and ministry. Of course, there is no one way to promote holiness; it appears differently among Christians and among church traditions. Some of the following sermons emphasize holiness broadly conceived, while others focus more narrowly on specific aspects of holy living. Other sermons barely mention the word holiness, yet they all reflect the call upon our lives to be holy, despite the variety of ways that exhortation occurs in our lives individually and collectively, socially and ministerially.

Scripture clearly says that it is not enough to be hearers of the word of God; we must also be doers of it. The apostle James says: "But be doers of the word, and not merely hearers who deceive themselves... But those who look into the perfect law, the law of liberty, and persevere, being not hearers who forget but doers who act—they will be blessed in their doing" (James 1:23, 25). Preaching holiness and pursuing it is not merely a pietistic or legalistic pipedream; on the contrary, it is liberating—by the grace of God—spiritually, physically, socially, and in every way imaginable.

God does not intend only to bless people spiritually with eternal life. God also wants to bless people here and now who, by faith, grow into greater likeness with Jesus Christ, resulting in love for God with all of one's heart, soul, mind, and strength, and love for one's neighbor as for oneself.

Theory and Practice

When I preach and teach, I emphasize the importance of Christians considering both the *theory and practice* of their Christianity. *Theory* has to do with the beliefs and values they have. *Practice* has to do with the applications of those beliefs in values in their lives—individually and collectively, spiritually and physically, ministerially and socially.

In order to do justice to the theory and practice of biblical holiness, I categorized the sermons in ways that talk about its breadth and depth. Each part communicates how we, by God's grace, find *strength to be holy*:

1. Part 1 deals with the *Nature of Holiness*, which presents the foundations of what holy living means for biblical authors as well as for Christians today.
2. Part 2 focuses upon *Our Holy God*, and how God's holiness includes the compassion of God the Father, the servanthood of Jesus Christ, and the empowerment of the Holy Spirit.
3. Part 3 talks about the hope we have, first for salvation by grace through faith, and second through the continued gracious work of the Holy Spirit by which believers become more holy—more loving and Christlike: *Hope of Holiness*.
4. Part 4 emphasizes the *Pursuit of Holiness* and the importance of Christians' attitudes and actions in embodying the kind of virtuous living to which God calls us.
5. Part 5 elaborates upon *Holy Disciplines*, described in Scripture, which instruct Christians about how they are to put their beliefs and values into practice for the sake of holy living.
6. Part 6 asserts how holiness is not a reality intended for individuals alone, but how it impacts all dimensions

of our lives and relationships—spiritually, physically, morally, and socially: *Social Holiness*.

God intends that Christians live vibrant, holy lives here and now, and not only in eternity. The holiness to which God calls us impacts all dimensions of our lives. It is holistic, integrating and perfecting parts of our lives too often left unreconciled: spirit and body, grace and discipline, heart and mind, word of God and Christian ritual, quietness and activism, ministry and social advocacy. It is our prayer and hope that readers of these sermons will become more informed and devoted to the embodiment of biblical holiness to which God calls us.

Part 1

Nature of Holiness

Sermon 1

Holiness Is What We Long For

By Don Thorsen

> Instead, as he who called you is holy, be holy yourselves in all your conduct; for it is written, "You shall be holy, for I am holy" (1 Peter 1:15-16, NRSV).

"Holiness, holiness is what I long for; holiness is what I need," are the words of a popular chorus sung in churches today, written by Micah Stampley. He continues, "Holiness, holiness is what You want for me." The longing for holiness that people have is not a recent development. Three hundred years ago, Charles Wesley penned the following words of a hymn: "Calm, O calm my troubled breast; Let me gain that second rest; From my works for ever cease, Perfected in holiness."

Throughout church history, Christians in particular have confessed their longing for biblical holiness—for the holiness that only God by grace through faith makes available to us. According to Scripture, God represents the purest embodiment of holiness: "Holy, holy, holy is the Lord of hosts; the whole earth is full of his glory" (Isaiah 6:3).

On the other hand, people are not holy, due to the effects of sin in their lives, individually and collectively. Yet, through the atonement of Jesus Christ, God views people as if they are holy because of Jesus' provision for their salvation. Through faith and repentance, people receive the gift of eternal life.

But God is not concerned only with people's eternal life after death; God is also concerned about their lives here and now. Holiness—or holy living—has to do with God's call for us to be holy, to love God and one's neighbor as oneself, to be Christ-like. 1 Peter 1:13-16 says:

> Therefore prepare your minds for action; discipline yourselves; set all your hope on the grace that Jesus Christ will bring you when he is revealed. Like obedient children, do not be conformed to the desires that you formerly had in ignorance. Instead, as he who called you is holy, be holy yourselves in all your conduct; for it is written, 'You shall be holy, for I am holy.'

Although Christians are saved by grace through faith, God calls everyone to live holy lives in order that they—by grace—may love God with their whole heart, soul, mind, and strength, and may love their neighbor as themselves. Let me begin by talking about the nature of holiness to which God calls us. I will continue by talking about how God intends for Christians to have the strength to be holy, and I will conclude by talking about how hopeful they should be for becoming holy in this life.

The Holiness to Which God Calls Us

John Wesley—the brother of Charles, and co-founder of the Methodist revival—had much to say about holiness. Yet, too many people nowadays, including Christians, unfortunately have a caricatured view of holy living. Holiness is thought of as legalistic, following a list of do's-and-don'ts, which has little to do with how Scripture talks about holy living.

Wesley believed that holiness primarily had to do with love. He thought that Jesus spoke in terms of love and its many implications, and thus holiness should be understood as loving, relational, and dynamic. A static list of how to live and how not to live captures a glimpse of the quality of relationships that God intends for people to have. But the more we focus upon the loving and relational dynamics of biblical holiness, the closer we will embody it.

Jesus said that the greatest commandment consists primarily of love. Consider Jesus' description of the "first" or "greatest commandment" in Mark 12:28-31:

> Jesus answered, "The first is, 'Hear, O Israel: the Lord our God, the Lord is one; you shall love the Lord your God with all your heart, and with all your soul, and with all your mind, and with all your strength'. The second is this, 'You shall love your neighbour as yourself'. There is no other commandment greater than these."

Wesley also thought of spiritual growth in Christians primarily in terms of love. Such love expectedly results in a lifestyle characterized by the many virtues described in Scripture. For example, Paul talks about "fruit of the Spirit," consisting of "love, joy, peace, patience, kindness, generosity, faithfulness, gentleness, and self-control" (Galatians 5:22-23). But at the heart of these virtues lies a life of love: toward God, self, and neighbor. After all, one cannot love one's neighbor as oneself without first appropriately loving oneself.

Elsewhere in Scripture, holy living is described as Christ-likeness, that is, living like Jesus. If we want to live obedient lives as Christians, then we should seek to emulate Jesus. That emulation has to do with more than occasionally asking the question, "What would Jesus do?" This question was famously penned by Charles Sheldon in a nineteenth century novel entitled *In His Steps*. Instead we should seek to emulate Jesus daily in *all* that we are, think, say, and do. As we yield to the presence and power of the Holy Spirit's gracious work in our lives, we may more and more live like Jesus, knowing better how he would act in any situation.

How Do We Become More Holy?

One of the most perplexing questions that I have asked myself is, "How do I become more holy?" Or, "How do I grow spiritually?" Such questions have become more troubling when people come to me, sometimes with great anguish, asking, "How may I grow as a Christian?"

Realistically, there is no single answer to this question. People's context is so particular that we need to be sensitive to the situatedness of their present circumstances, the place in their spiritual journey, their temperament, emotional strengths and weaknesses, and so on. In addition, Scripture does not provide one single way to grow spiritually. On the contrary, it contains a rich variety of ways—or means—by which God graciously works in people's lives.

Sometimes people in general, and Christians in particular, become confused about the means by which spiritual growth occurs. Out of fear of works-righteousness, they react (or overreact) by doing nothing, claiming that God alone is responsible for their *sanctification*, that is, the conforming of people to Christ-likeness. Too many lack hope for the restoration of the image of God in their lives that became distorted due to the past and present effects of sin.

However, God never intended that Christians should live lives of passivity, mistakenly thinking that biblical allusions to "wait for the Lord" (Isaiah 40:31) or "rest in the Lord" (Psalm 37:7) meant that they do nothing. Since Old Testament times, God repeatedly engaged people in covenantal relationships. Although God may guarantee the ultimate (or eternal) benefits of these covenants with people, God still held them responsible. How else do we account for sin, if not for the genuine moral choices people make? How else do we account for the judgment of sin and evil that Scripture describes? The concepts of personal responsibility and moral accountability make no sense, if God has made no provision for people's freedom to choose.

Throughout church history, Christians have often been perplexed about the role God plays in their lives, on the one hand, and the role of people, on the other hand. I think that people have an innate craving for meaning, and the hope that everything has an ultimate reason—an ultimate divine cause (even for sin, evil, pain, and suffering). Yet Scripture repeatedly says that people have responsibility for decisions they make here and now; they have sufficient freedom to choose. This freedom may be limited, of course, due to human finitude, cultural influences, and the effects of sin. But by grace, people are still accountable to believe, to hope, to love—to be holy.

John Wesley talked about human freedom and responsibility as "free grace" (*Free Grace*). In other words, people have no innate human power to save themselves or to grow in holiness. Yet, by the grace of God, people may (and must) make consequential decisions in this life, indeed even about their eternal life. To be sure, God graciously initiates, empowers, and completes our salvation. But in that process, God's grace works preveniently (or in advance), providing people sufficient freedom to decide for themselves. That freedom, enabled by prevenient grace, impacts not only our decisions to accept God's gift of eternal life; it also impacts our decisions to grow in grace through the presence and power of the Holy Spirit.

The apostle Paul perceptively captures this process of spiritual growth with an analogy of planting and watering seeds. In 1 Corinthians 3:6, he says: "I planted, Apollos watered, but God gave the growth." Although God gives the spiritual growth, people are not without appropriate responsibilities and roles. God wants to partner with people both for their salvation and for their growth in holiness, love, and Christ-likeness.

Ultimately, there remain mysteries with regard to all the spiritual workings of God and God's grace in our lives. Yet we may remain very hopeful about how God can and does work in the world in general, and in people in particular. Just as Christians believe that our sovereign God has the power to create the world, save us from sin and death, and perform miracles, God continues to work powerfully in the lives of Christians for their sanctification—their progressive growth in holiness, love, and Christ-likeness.

By What Means Do We Become Holy?

Scripture mentions various ways or means by which Christians may grow in grace, grow in love, and become more like Jesus Christ. In history, various church traditions arose that emphasized different parts of Scripture for the sake of spiritual formation. Let me summarize some of the more prominent approaches to Christian spirituality.

1. *Evangelical* church traditions believe that the height of holy living has to do with proclamation of the gospel message of Jesus Christ. They focus on evangelization, missions, and church planting.

2. *Sacramental* church traditions believe that the height of holy living has to do with public worship. They focus on praising God with music, singing, and liturgy, usually including celebration of the sacraments.
3. *Contemplative* church traditions believe that the height of holy living has to do with practice of the spiritual disciplines. According to Dallas Willard, such practices include spiritual disciplines of engagement (e.g., prayer, study, worship, fellowship, service) as well as spiritual disciplines of abstinence (e.g., silence, solitude, fasting, meditation, contemplation) (*The Spirit of the Disciplines*).
4. *Studious* church traditions believe that the height of holy living has to do with the study of Scripture. They focus on reading, interpreting, applying, teaching, defending, and proclaiming the whole of Scripture.
5. *Holiness* church traditions believe that the height of holy living has to do with discipleship and the embodiment of the virtues, or "fruit of the Spirit" (Galatians 5:22-23). My personal church background comes from the holiness tradition, and I think it captures well the holistic dimensions of holy living. At the same time, I acknowledge the variety of biblical teachings about spiritual formation and of the ways that Christians historically pursued holiness, which represent equally valid ways of loving God and others.
6. *Activist* church traditions believe that the height of holy living has to do with caring for the poor, healing the sick, and housing the homeless. Such compassion ministries should be supplemented by advocacy ministries on behalf of social justice, equal opportunities, and peacemaking.
7. *Charismatic* church traditions believe that the height of holy living has to do with the discovery, development, and use of one's spiritual gifts (or charisms). Such use of spiritual gifts builds up the church and individuals as well as minister to others.
8. *Ecumenical* church traditions believe that the height of holy living has to do with finding ways for Christians and churches to cooperate in ministry and perhaps join togeth-

er. They endeavor to embody Jesus' prayer that his disciples "may all be one" (John 17:21).

Other church traditions could be added to the ones listed above. The list is not exhaustive. But each tradition in its own way seeks to embody biblical holiness, even if that particular phraseology is not regularly used. All of them contribute to holiness, holistically conceived, which is seldom embodied in a single Christian, church, or denomination. Yet all of them serve as the "body of Christ," representing symbolically the head, hands, and feet of the church, which Paul describes as equally valuable and necessary for ministering effectively in the world (1 Corinthians 12:12-26).

How Hopeful of Holiness Are We to Be?

The book of Zechariah tells an inspiring story of how the Israelites persevered through conquest by foreign military powers, which killed, dispersed, and enslaved the people of Israel. Yet, Zechariah describes the Israelites as "prisoners of hope," because of their belief that God will be faithful and ultimately victorious, despite temporal confusion, pain, and suffering (Zechariah 9:12).

Likewise, Jesus was hopeful with regard to the degree of maturity and ministry that his followers may achieve. In the middle of his so-called *Sermon on the Mount* (Matthew 5-7), Jesus made an audacious exhortation: "Be perfect, therefore, as your heavenly Father is perfect" (Matthew 5:48). This statement has been interpreted several ways by Christians, but it cannot be denied that Jesus' *telos* or goal was for his followers to become increasingly like him—loving, caring for the poor, healing the sick, casting out demons, and proclaiming the gospel (or good news) of eternal life (e.g., Luke 4:16-21).

Even the apostle Paul gave reasons to be optimistic about the degree to which we may expect to become holy in this life. Despite his realism about the effects of sin (e.g., Romans 7:14-25), he believed that Christians are "more than conquerors through him who loved us" (Romans 8:37). Paul's hopefulness culminates in the following exhortation: "May the God of peace himself sanctify you entirely; and may your spirit and soul and body be kept sound and blameless at the coming of our Lord Jesus Christ. The one who calls you is faithful, and he will do this" (1 Thessalonians 5:23-24).

John Wesley is among the most prominent "prisoners of hope" with regard to the degree to which Christians, by God's grace, may find the strength to be holy. He used the language of "entire sanctification" and even "Christian perfection" to describe his hopefulness (*A Plain Account of Christian Perfection*). Regrettably, such phraseology has been misunderstood by some people, thinking that Wesley advocated the possibility of absolute sinlessness. Of course, he advocated no such thing. Wesley thought of holiness in positive terms of love, more than negative terms of avoiding sin. If Jesus told people to love God and their neighbors as themselves, then Wesley believed that such love was possible and desirable, and by the grace of God, that Christ-likeness should be pursued.

When I talk about Wesley's view of holiness and sanctification, I refer to the commonplace references that Christians often make to Jesus as their *Savior* and *Lord*. Usually when people convert to Christianity, we say that Jesus then became their Savior. Yet, in their lives, Jesus may not yet have become their Lord. To be sure, Jesus is Lord of the universe, but ordinarily new believers do not consecrate their lives wholly to God until sometime subsequent to their conversion. When that consecration occurs in which Christians present their "bodies as a living sacrifice, holy and acceptable to God" (Romans 12:1), then Jesus wholly becomes their Lord and Savior.

Consecrating oneself to the lordship of Jesus Christ is not a one-time event. It represents a life of commitment, a life of relationship, a life of love. If love is the ultimate expression of holiness, then it is because salvation is essentially relational in nature. Salvation is to be understood as reconciliation with God our maker, our parent—one with whom we may grow in intimacy, fellowship, and blessing. Likewise holiness is to be understood as a loving relationship, based on faith and hope, which includes love for God, love for ourselves, and love for others. Such love cares not only for one another's spiritual well-being, but for their holistic well-being—physically, emotionally, relationally, and socially.

Conclusion

Is Jesus Christ both your Savior *and* Lord? Is Jesus Lord of your personal life, values, and plans for the future? Is Jesus Lord of your social life, in terms of how you relate with your neighbor justly, economically, and politically as well as interpersonally? Do you embody Jesus' compassion and advocacy for the poor as well as for the proclamation of the gospel?

I began this sermon with the words of a chorus: "Holiness, holiness is what I long for." I believe that God has created us to be holy, to be like Jesus—as we were originally created in the image of God. Despite our finite and sinful endeavors to resist holiness, God's Spirit preveniently instills within us the desire to be holy. Such a desire is fulfilled initially with our acceptance of Jesus as our Savior. But our desire for holiness can only be fulfilled in this life as we daily submit ourselves to the lordship of Jesus. Through the amazing, gracious power of the Holy Spirit, we should be hopeful and expectant of the ever deepening ways in which we may express love to God, and to our neighbors as to ourselves. Amen.

Sermon 2

The Holy River of God

Kevin W. Mannoia

Ezekiel 47:1-9

There is a river—it is the river of God. It is the river of God's holiness. It runs broad and fast through the desert land of the world. It doesn't begin in the church, nor in the councils, nor in the books of order or discipline. It doesn't even begin with the bishop or the statements of doctrine. And thankfully it doesn't begin in any board or committees. Whether there is a bishop or no bishop, the river still flows. This river begins in the temple—the very heart of God—and flows freely throughout the land. Like any river, this river is always moving, always changing, and always life-giving.

A river by definition moves. It flows. When a river stops moving, it ceases to be a river and turns into a stagnant swamp. It becomes smelly and attracts only the mosquitos. This river of holiness that flows from the very heart of God is always moving. Those found within it will always be carried to places they did not expect, never stagnant, never arriving, and never stopped in the achievement of some particular level of growth or service.

As well, a river by definition always changes. From one year to the next, the banks of the river will wash away, changing the contour and path of the river. Over the course of time, the river will change in its course, and the scenery along the side will be changed by it. Those found within its flow will also find they are always changing, never set in one particular path but dynamically adjusting to the circumstances about them.

A river is always life-giving. Like the images from space of the Nile River, every river brings lush, green life along its edges—wherever it goes, life swarms. It transforms the dry arid land into fruit bearing land that sustains life. Those found within it will bring the life-giving water to the crevices and arid places in the desolate and abandoned corners of the world.

But this river is not of our creation. Yet we may participate in it. In fact our immersion in it adds to the flow and influence it carries as it brings life from the very heart of God to the dryness of the world. And it is into this river that, like Ezekiel, we are invited to participate.

Imagine the River with Two Parts

Imagine the river with two parts: The banks made of dirt, which are the worldly dimensions of our own security, ambitions, agendas, and selfish plans; and secondly the water, which is the life-giving flow of God's holy nature flowing from His very heart in vulnerable love through the world He seeks to restore.

Ezekiel is invited by the guide to leave the banks—the dirt, the sand—and come into the river of God's holiness. He accepts the invitation, as many of us do, and enters ankle deep. He is in the river, no doubt. But his feet remain firmly planted in the dirt at the bottom—like many who say yes to Jesus and who are without a doubt in the river of God. But fearful of giving up too much, they remain in the shallows where their feet are firmly planted in the security of their own devising—their own agendas, plans, ambitions, and destiny. There is no question that they are in the river. But also completely controlling their life.

The guide invites again. And a second time Ezekiel accepts the invitation. This time it is to go deeper. Now the flow is up to his knees. Deeper and more committed. Perhaps for the Christ-follower this is a choice to take on newer responsibilities or deeper surrender. The water begins to have more of an effect. Like standing at the sea with waves crashing around your feet, soon the rushing water of the river begins to wash away the dirt from under your feet. The erosion is the Spirit attempting to encourage total dependence and surrender to the flow of God's holiness. And as the dirt is washed from under our feet, we grow less stable and confident in our stance. In human fashion that does not like to lose control, we lift our feet and place them in a fresh, new location on the bottom of the river where we once again are stable and solidly in control of our own destiny and balance. We are in the river, but with our feet firmly planted in the dirt at the bottom. Again, working hard to remain balanced and in control of our own life.

Another invitation to go deeper takes the prophet in waist deep. Now the current of the river is strong. So strong that it requires you to broaden your stance and resist the pressure on you as it splashes and pushes against you. That is the holy flow of God seeking your surrender to allow the Spirit to carry you. Yet again your stance remains fixed against the flow: Rooted firmly in the dirt at the bottom; maintaining selfish resistance to the pressure of the Holy Spirit. Oh yes, you are in the river. Deep in the river. Perhaps leading small groups, discipling others, teaching classes, and devoting time to be with God. But the foundation of your life and the destiny of your will remain solidly in your control with your feet planted in the dirt at the bottom of the river.

Finally the invitation comes again to go deeper. This time it is so deep that it is uncrossable. It's over your head. As you walk in further, the water gets higher and higher to the point where you are no longer able to keep your feet on the bottom and your head above water at the same time. By accepting the invitation to go into the deep you come to a choice. That critical point comes when you must decide: Do you let your feet leave the security of your own control and trust the water to sustain you, or do you turn back to the shallows where you maintain complete control with your feet on the bottom? That is the choice of your life.

The Choice of Your Life

You're on your tip toes trying every option to maintain just a touch on the bottom where you feel you are in control. And the awesome reality bears upon you—to let go, or to turn back. Is it frightening? Yes indeed. Is it a hard choice? You bet. To be carried fully and completely in the flow of God's holiness or to keep your feet on the bottom where at least you have the security of controlling your own formation and destiny; that is the choice that must be made.

As you finally make that deep, soul-surrendering choice to let your feet come off the bottom, you find that the holy flow of God's heart bears you up, carrying you in the redemptive restoration of His love. And suddenly as you surrender to the flow and release control, you find things changing completely.

Until now, with your feet planted in the dirt at the bottom of the river, you have remained fixed in your own self-determined position watching as the river goes by. But now, as your feet come off the bottom, you are carried along in the flow of the river watching as the banks slide by. And the pressure against your side subsides as the river takes you with it.

You have not created this river, for it flows from the very heart of God. But in its flow you are carried to places that are dry and desert, needy and broken, hurting and lost. And there, you bring life, and renewal, and grace, and peace, and love. Perhaps at the office, or perhaps at school. Maybe with your family members or neighbors. Or even in the casual encounters of your day. Wherever you go, you bring life—the life of God's holiness transforming the desert into lush, life-sustaining land. Restoring the land of one person's heart, or the community, or the church, or the city, or the workplace closer to what God envisioned from the beginning.

You may not be alone in bringing life for there are many in this river. But you are part of its current. And you know that the river flows ahead of you as well as behind you. Others have brought life before you, and others will follow after. In this flow we are always moving and always leaving a changed environment.

You do not know where it goes. But that is not as important as the fact that, wherever the river goes, it brings life. And in your surrendered release, you help in bringing the restoration of transformation wherever you go.

But there is a warning. As with any river, there are some places that become traps. On occasion as the water begins to swirl in a small eddy of self-indulgence, the interaction with the dirt on the banks brings confusion. Perhaps you have walked close to the edge of a river and found the soft places where the water and the dirt are mixed. It is no longer only water, and no longer only dirt. It has become confused so that it is no longer either, but really both. It's muddy, squishy, and mucky.

The identity confusion resulting from this syncretism prevents the free flow and movement of the river. Certainly where the water gives itself to bring life, there is restoration of the land. But where there is careless toying in an effort to be both, the effect is overdone, and the land becomes useless and swampy. It does not really know what it is. Is it dirt? Not really. Is it water? Not completely. It is some confusing combination of the two that serves only as a quagmire to confuse and entrap. Be careful not to toy too much with being both water and dirt under the guise of relevance, for there is but one Lord and one master.

In the World, but Not of the World

Of course we know that we are called to be in the world. But also not of the world. This delicate balance of engagement and separateness is only achieved by allowing the very holy nature of God to be completely and wholly reflected in and through us. For God's holiness alone is truly capable of being reflected in that perfected balance of being wholly other, while also being responsibly engaged.

Any effort on our part to manage the intricate balance between the two by our own cleverness will always fall short and yield a legalistic bias toward one or the other—sectarianism or mere social activism. The act of release and surrender, allowing the holy river of God to completely carry us, is the singular act of our will. It allows God's nature to be naturally reflected so that His otherness yields the magnetic vision for a whole person and creation, and His engagement compels initiative in reaching the broken people and places of creation.

Lest we are distracted by the pitfalls of the swirling eddies, know that the river we have now surrendered to carries us through the needy places bringing life wherever it goes. There is fruit; there is transformation; there is wholeness as God intended. Be reminded that this river is not of our own doing. It is not the creation of any person or group. It comes from the very heart of God. It is not like other themes we embrace in Scripture that are about God's actions toward us, or in us, or through us. This river of holiness is the very nature of God, flowing from His heart. And so, wherever it goes there is life.

The question, then, is simple. Where are your feet planted? Perhaps you are in the river, but your feet are firmly secured in the dirt at the bottom, where you maintain control of your own destiny and agenda. You may even be quite deep in the river—committed to high levels of activity or leadership within the church of God. Yet you derive your security from your own ability to control and direct your will.

Perhaps you have even taken things into your own hands in an effort to become relevant and accepted by people. In the process, you find yourself in a sidelined whirlpool that increasingly is causing deep identity confusion in you. You wonder what difference it all makes anyway. You ask, "Is there really a transformation that is possible? Or, do we just reframe what we see in this world in a way that allows it to become Christian?" Whatever your place, wherever you are, the most important question remains: "Where are your feet planted?"

Where Are Your Feet Planted?

So I'd like to ask two questions:

1. If you are standing on the banks of the river and have never accepted the invitation to step into the water, would you accept that invitation now and step in?
2. If you are in the water—to your ankles, knees, or waist—but your feet remain securely lodged in the selfish security of your own will and destiny, and you'd like to accept the invitation to go in where your feet cannot touch bottom, then would you make that choice of surrender?

I assure you that the river of God's holiness will sustain you. It is a frightening act of surrender. But God has never failed to uphold, transform, and carry those who have faithfully let their feet come off the bottom and flow with the river of His holiness in complete surrender. It is a truly breath-taking choice. Where are your feet planted?

> *May the grace of God welcome you deep into the river of His holiness, carrying you in its flow, transforming you, and through you bringing the life of God's wholeness to broken people and places in His restorative love.*

Sermon 3

The Aroma of Holiness

Lynn Allan Losie

2 Corinthians 2:14-16

When we think of the seasons of the year, our minds often turn to the aromas or smells that we associate with them, even in southern California where the seasons are sometimes hard to distinguish from one another. In springtime, there might be the fragrant scent of blooming jasmine; in summer, there is the sweet and musty smell of salt and seaweed at the beach; autumn can bring the acrid fume of fire, as dry hillsides break out in flames, a reminder that smells can signal danger as well as soothe with pleasure; and winter, as elsewhere throughout the country, is enriched by burning candles, scented with cinnamon and spice.

We, of course, prefer pleasing smells to noxious ones, and we have whole industries dedicated to suppressing the odors of our humanity, especially in the United States. Our supermarkets and drug stores have shelves filled with deodorants, perfumes, body sprays, toothpastes, and mouthwashes, in forms we can even take with us for use during the day. Our fitness centers try hard, with high-powered ventilation systems, to reduce the smell of the sweat of bodies pumping iron and toiling on machines. Humanity apparently should be odorless.

But this has not always been the case, as documented by Katherine Ashenburg's fascinating book *The Dirt on Clean: An Unsanitized History*. Ashenburg recounts how for many centuries of Western civilization the air around humanity was pungent with smells and odors—even up to fairly modern times. As she begins her book, she tells a story about childhood memories of her grandmother, who was from Eastern Europe. Ashenburg recalls that her grandmother smelled like bread dough and something else, which as a child she called "grandmother smell." She couldn't put her finger on what it was. But when she visited Eastern Europe later in life, she discovered that the "grandmother smell" was all around her, and Ashenburg realized it had to do with a different standard of hygiene. This smell was not offensive to her when she was a child—it was simply the smell of her grandmother—but as an adult she had become more judgmental. The aroma of grandmother had become a stink.

The Smells of Holiness

If we think of holiness in terms of smells, then our first thought might be of a sweet fragrance—"a fragrant offering, a sacrifice acceptable and pleasing to God" (Philippians 4:18, NRSV). Holiness is something pure; it suggests the perfume of incense, the smell of something made clean. And this is one of the biblical images of holiness. As the prophet Ezekiel looks to the future and the fulfillment of the promise of the restoration of Israel, he presents a vision of God's redeemed people as a "pleasing odor" to God (Ezekiel 20:40-41):

> For on my holy mountain, the mountain height of Israel, says the Lord God, there all the house of Israel, all of them, shall serve me in the land; there I will accept them, and there I will require your contributions and the choicest of your gifts, with all your sacred things. As a pleasing odor I will accept you, when I bring you out from the peoples, and gather you out of the countries where you have been scattered; and I will manifest my holiness among you in the sight of the nations.

In the prophet's vision, when God's redeemed people worship him in the proper place (his "holy mountain") with proper offerings (their "sacred [or holy] things"), they are accepted as the "pleasing odor" of sacrifice. Dedicated worship honoring God the redeemer is a fragrance, and it is a fragrance through which God "manifests his holiness"—through which God's supremacy over his people and the world becomes known.

In 2 Corinthians 2:14-16, however, the Apostle Paul uses the image of the smell of sacrifice in a different way. He speaks of the Christian life—a life dedicated in holy service to God—in terms of contrasting smells, and they are not all sweet:

> But thanks be to God, who in Christ always leads us in triumphal procession, and through us spreads in every place the fragrance that comes from knowing him. For we are the aroma of Christ to God among those who are being saved and among those who are perishing; to the one a fragrance from death to death, to the other a fragrance from life to life.

Paul here is using the imagery of a Roman triumphal procession, which would have concluded at a sacrificial altar in the center of the city. As the procession would wend its way through the streets, the city would be filled with the smell of burning incense, and then as it came to a halt at the capitol, there would be the odor of the sacrifices that would be offered in thanksgiving to the gods. For the victors these smells would be the fragrance of triumph, but for the vanquished they would be the stench of death, as the leaders of those who had been conquered would meet their ultimate fate.

In the city of Rome today, on the *Via Sacra* just to the southeast of the Roman Forum, there is a huge stone monument known as the Arch of Titus. It was constructed in A.D. 82 by the Emperor Domitian in honor of the triumph of the Emperor Titus, who with his father, the Emperor Vespasian, had crushed the Jewish revolt against the Romans in A.D. 70. In the Roman conquest, Jerusalem was burned and "not one stone was left upon another" in the Temple, as Jesus had predicted (Mark 13:2). Reliefs on the arch portray the triumphal procession of Titus into the city, with laurel-crowned attendants carrying the spoils of war—the sacred Menorah and the Table of the Bread of the Presence from the Holy Place in the Temple in Jerusalem, and the silver trumpets that called the Jewish people to rejoice in the New Year. The Arch of Titus commemorates a great celebration, but it is also a reminder that the Jewish people suffered great devastation.

Not only is this momentous event preserved in stone, but it is also recounted by the first-century Jewish historian Josephus in his book *The Jewish War*, which gives us one of the most complete accounts of what a Roman triumph was like. Here is some of what he reports:

> It is impossible to give a satisfactory account of the innumerable spectacles... showing forth the greatness of the Roman Empire.... Furthermore, not even the host of captives went unadorned.... Numbers of tableaux showed the successive stages of the war most vividly portrayed. Here was to be seen a smiling countryside laid waste, there whole formations of the enemy put to the sword...the whole place reeking of slaughter....

> Most of the spoils that were carried were heaped up indiscriminately, but more prominent than all the rest were those captured in the Temple at Jerusalem.... Next came a large group carrying images of Victory.... Behind them drove Vespasian first with Titus behind him....

> The procession finished at the Temple of Jupiter on the Capitol, where they came to a halt: it was an ancient custom to wait there till news came that the commander-in-chief of the enemy was dead. This was Simon, son of Gioras, who had been marching in the procession among the prisoners.... When the news of his end arrived it was received with universal acclamation, and the sacrifices were begun.... All day long the City of Rome celebrated the triumphant issue of the campaign against her enemies, the end of civil strife, and the beginning of hope for a joyful future (Josephus, *Jewish War*).

As we can see from this account by Josephus, the smell of sacrifices began to waft through the city when the execution of the revolutionary leader Simon was announced. The smell of "hope for a joyful future" for Rome was the smell of death for the conquered Jewish people.

The Aroma of Christ

Paul picks up the imagery of the Roman triumph, and the smells associated with it, to show how sacrificial service to God, in holy dedication to Jesus Christ, means both life and death. Christians are pictured as being led by Christ in a triumphal procession as those who have been conquered by him, but they are also following a Christ who himself was "obedient to the point of death—even death on a cross" (Philippians 2:8). So, as Paul says later in his Second Letter to the Corinthians, Christians are "always carrying in the body the death of Jesus, so that the life of Jesus may also be made visible in our bodies" (2 Corinthians 4:10). This means that the "aroma of Christ" that is part of the triumphal procession—the smell of holy dedication to Christ—is a fragrance, but a fragrance that is at the same time the perfume of life and the stench of death.

We don't yet have a "scratch and sniff" Bible, but if we did, following Jesus around on his tour of Galilee would plunge us into a world of foul odors. Jesus touches a leper, perhaps who had oozing sores (Mark 1:40-45); he is grasped by a woman with a flow of blood, who had been suffering from this malady for twelve years (Mark 5:25-34); he is embraced by a blind beggar, who had been sitting outside, beside the road, and who throws off his coat and comes to him (Mark 10:46-52); and he asks to see a man who had been in the grave for four days. Just imagine for a moment what it meant for Jesus to command the mourners at the tomb of Lazarus to remove stone. Martha, the sister of Lazarus, is aghast, and exclaims, "Lord, by this time he stinketh" (John 11:39, KJV). But Jesus did not try to avoid the smells of humanity, the smells of sickness and death. He was the one who was born in a stable (Luke 2:7), and he was the one who did not wash his hands (Luke 11:37-41), who did not cleanse himself from the odors of the world around him.

What then is the "aroma of Christ" about which Paul speaks? What is the smell of a holy life dedicated to God? It is the smell of humanity—the smell of toil and labor, the smell of illness, and the smell of death. It is the smell of the incarnation—the en-flesh-ment—of the one who took on our humanity and sweat like drops of blood as he agonized in the garden in contemplation of God's will that would take him to the cross (Luke 22:44). This means that, for Christians who bear witness to Christ, it is taking on the smell of the other, reaching out beyond our own sanitized zone of comfort to identify with anyone in need of God's redeeming grace.

A few decades ago, at the conclusion of the Vietnam War, many refugees were flooding into the United States from Southeast Asia, and churches were reaching out to these new arrivals in ministries to meet their physical and spiritual needs. My father was talking with a pastor who was working with the Hmong people from Cambodia and was struck by the pastor's remark that the newly arrived Cambodians thought that Americans smelled like cows. My father was surprised; he thought of other cultures in terms of smells, but he didn't realize that he also had an odor. We don't notice our own smell—our own humanity—but we notice the smells of difference. We not only are what we eat, but we smell like what we eat—and who we are and what we do. Often our tendency is to want to sanitize and remove the smells that offend us. But as we reach down and touch the humanity of those in need, the stench that we acquire will become the "aroma of Christ," which to God is a sweet fragrance of frankincense and myrrh.

Conclusion

In Paul's Letter to the Romans, he appeals to us as followers of Jesus Christ to "present [our] bodies a living sacrifice, holy, acceptable unto God, which is [our] reasonable service" (Romans 12:1, KJV). What is the smell of this life offered in the sacrifice of service? What is the "aroma of Christ" that we as Christians spread to the world? What is the smell of holiness? We might think of it as disinfecting ourselves in order to be what we consider to be something sweet and pleasant to the world. We might think of being called to be God's "Febreze." But God has a different sense of smell; through the incarnation of his Son, Jesus Christ, he took on the "grandmother smell"—the smell of humanity, the smell of death, which was ultimately the smell of love. We as Christians are called to do the same: "Therefore be imitators of God, as beloved children, and live in love, as Christ loved us and gave himself up for us, a fragrant offering and sacrifice to God" (Ephesians 5:1-2, NRSV).

Part 2

Our Holy God

Sermon 4

The Holy God of Compassionate Power

Tony Baron

Soon afterwards he went to a town called Nain, and his disciples and a large crowd went with him. As he approached the gate of the town, a man who had died was being carried out. He was his mother's only son, and she was a widow; and with her was a large crowd from the town. When the Lord saw her, he had compassion for her and said to her, "Do not weep." Then he came forward and touched the bier, and the bearers stood still. And he said, "Young man, I say to you, rise! " The dead man sat up and began to speak, and Jesus gave him to his mother. Fear seized all ot them; and they glorified God, saying, "A great prophet has risen among us!" and "God has looked favorably on his people!" This word about him spread through Judea and all the surrounding country (Luke 7:11-17, NRSV).

Death. It's hard, isn't it?
 When people we love lose their life on earth, we are left to suffer the loss. Even when we are certain that they are with their heavenly Father, we still experience a profound loss of those people, of those relation-

ships. We grieve that they are no longer a living breathing part of our lives. It is painful.

One of my dearest mentors passed away on May 8, 2013. Dallas Willard, a Professor of Philosophy at USC and noted author on spiritual formation, was my Doctoral Professor at Fuller Theological Seminary. He was more than a teacher and mentor. Dallas was truly a spiritual father to me—a guide for holiness, love, and compassion. And now he is gone. And, it's painful.

Although I knew Dallas was close to taking his last breath on earth, I vividly remember how hard it hit me when I received word about his death. I thought I would be prepared. But how can one truly be prepared? Even though he was ready to meet his maker, I was not ready for him to leave.

Dallas had suffered from pancreatic cancer, the same disease that took my father fifteen years earlier. At his memorial service everyone was tearful, even though we knew where Dallas was now, and to whom he belonged. Though the service was a celebration of his life, we all shared a very real poignant sense of loss because our mentor was no longer here with us. We missed him deeply.

As a pastor, I have been acquainted with death more times than I care to think about. I have had conversations with many who have tragically and unexpectedly lost loved ones. When we experience that kind of loss, we seem to lose a piece of ourselves with them. When we lose someone dear to us, for a brief period of time our priorities and perspectives change. Momentarily, our routines change, and we see life through a wide-angle lens. In these moments of grief, we realize how precious life truly is.

God is not untouched by our grief. In the Gospel of Luke, we begin at a place of heart-breaking loss. A widow is grieving the death of her son. She has lost her husband in the past, and now her only son. She is numb, hurting, and may not realize it yet—but in all likelihood, she has also lost her only means of financial support.

Can you imagine the depths of her despair? In the context of her story, God begins to teach us about Himself. He is not insensitive to our sorrows. No, His heart is for us, and He understands what it means to live a holy life in a fragile world. He wants to tell us what He is like as a Father to us. He wants to have an intimate relationship with us, his children.

The Context to Inspire Us

Perhaps a little bit of context will be helpful. The author Luke is thought to be the only Gentile writer of all the authors in the New Testament. Luke decided that he would not write just one book, but two. We can't really understand the full intention of Luke in his Gospel unless we also read the second volume, the book of Acts. Reading both books means we are reading nearly twenty-five percent of the New Testament. Scholars believe that Luke, being a medical doctor, may have studied medicine in Tarsus, while the apostle Paul studied philosophy and theology in the same city.

It was a priority to Luke to be meticulous. So he secured information directly from eyewitnesses and writings from other reliable resources (Luke 1:1-3). Additionally, we know that Luke and the apostle Paul spent significant time together. In the book of Acts, we begin to see the term *we* as Luke describes his missionary travels with Paul. We know the two men were close friends. Paul, in 2 Timothy 4:11, describes Luke as the only one who has stayed with him during his imprisonment. In Colossians 4:14, Paul calls Luke "a dear friend."

In the book of Luke, and Acts as well, 800 new Greek words are used that are never used in the New Testament! It is clearly a depiction of someone highly educated like Luke who was being intentionally accurate and eloquent in what he wanted to relay to Theophilos, the person to whom Luke dedicated his writings. But what strikes me about everything else I read in the Gospel of Luke is his unrelenting interest in the life of Jesus to the marginalized and the dispossessed, many of whom desired to live holy lives but felt unworthy. The feelings of unworthiness were often caused by the difficult circumstances of life, personal misdirected choices, and the critical judgments by those in positions of authority.

Luke places substantial emphasis on God's love for the outsider of the religious inner circle—children, the poor, tax collectors, the outcasts, the sinners, women, Samaritans, and Gentiles. Luke wanted the reader to know confidently that Jesus cares profoundly for the rejected and the dejected. He wanted to make it crystal clear that God is deeply invested in those who feel marginalized by the power structure of the world. Luke wanted to communicate that these people are not overlooked. Rather, they are infinitely important in the eyes of God.

The Biblical Text to Equip Us

You can see why I love this book so much! When we come to the story in the seventh chapter of Luke, a fundamental question is developing. And that is: Who is Jesus?

The seventh chapter ties into the question that John the Baptist poses to Jesus, "Are you the one who is to come, or are we to wait for another?" (Luke 7:19). And Luke answers that very question in the seventh chapter. Jesus responds, "Go and tell John what you have seen and heard: the blind receive their sight, the lame walk, the lepers are cleansed, the deaf hear, the dead are raised, the poor have good news brought to them. And blessed is anyone who takes no offense at me" (Luke 7:22-23).

Who is the only one that can heal the sick by just speaking the word? Read Luke 7:1-10 where Jesus heals a centurion's servant by just speaking a word. The answer is Jesus. In Luke 7:46-49, we find a condemned woman who is passionately anointing Jesus' feet and drying them with her hair. Jesus is moved with compassion and forgives her sins. Who forgives sins? The answer is Jesus—the only one who can forgive sins.

Finally, in verses 11-17, we come upon this unusual passage. It is not found in any other Gospel account. And the question is, "Who is this that can bring the dead to life?" The answer again is Jesus.

It is Jesus who can heal the sick just by saying a word; it is Jesus who can forgive sins when no one else can. It is Jesus who can bring the dead to life. And Luke wanted to make it clear who this Jesus is. He is God. His demonstration of healing, of forgiveness, of restoring life is so much more than a public display of His awesome power. It is an outward expression of His deep, passionate love. Our Father has a fierce love for His children. He is showing us that He is touched by our infirmities, compassionate about our failures, and deeply moved by our sorrows.

Now, picture this with me. The miracle of the Samaritan servant was in Capernaum twenty-five miles away. So following that beautiful miracle there, Jesus with a very large crowd, walks twenty-five miles to the city of Nain. By early afternoon, here comes this joyful procession approaching the city gates. They were possibly laughing and joking. They were telling stories. They were thinking how wonderful life is! And there must have been this shared sense of how miraculous it was that they were following the Messiah!

But beginning in verse eleven, Luke says, "as He approached the gate of the town a man who had died was being carried out." So, *outside* the city gate this jubilant procession of people is approaching with Jesus. But *inside* of the city gate, a much different procession is approaching. There is a widow suffering the unspeakable loss of her only child. No husband with whom to share her grief. She is alone. She is heart-broken.

On the funeral side, as was customary, the crowd was filled with musicians playing their flutes and cymbals. As was also the custom, the grieving family, in this case a widow, would also hire professional mourners to wail and cry. And at the city gate these two processions collide. There is music, laughter, wailing, children, and adults intersecting and making their way through the city gate in opposite directions. And in the midst of this commotion, Jesus saw the widow and, moved with compassion, consoled her saying, "Do not weep" (Luke 7:13).

There was a collision of life and death. Joy and despair. Hope and hopelessness. Compassion and grief.

God Has Compassion for Us in This life

What happens when life and death meet? God sees. He is moved with compassion. And He reaches out to our hearts with the love of a Father.

Dallas Willard used to teach me and others never to forget that God is always good. He said to me that he knows the world can confuse us at times. You look at the world, and many aspects of it seem awful. Sometimes it may even feel like God doesn't care, but it is not true. For our God is always good.

One reason the seventh chapter of Luke was given to us under the inspiration of God was to communicate to us how much He cares. When we are hurting, He is not distant and untouched by our pain.

He is moved with compassion. And compassion moves Him to action. He heals. He forgives. He restores life.

The word *passion* literally means "to suffer." When you have passion for something, as illustrated in Mel Gibson's movie *The Passion of the Christ*, it means having a *suffering* experience. So the idea of having *passion* means to *suffer*. In the word *compassion*, the prefix means to have passion *with*. So this passage means that Jesus was *suffering with* the widow as she grieved the loss of her only son.

There are only two other times in the New Testament that this particular word is used, and both times are in the Gospel of Luke. It is used once in Luke 10:33, in the passage we often call the parable of the Good Samaritan. Remember the violent mugging that took place and the various responses?

Jesus offers the story of the Good Samaritan in response to an attorney who is testing Jesus with the question, "What must I do to inherit eternal life?" (Luke 10:25). Jesus answers the question with a question in verse 26, "What is written in the law?" The attorney correctly replies by quoting Scripture in the next verse, "You shall love the Lord your God with all your heart, with all your soul, and with all your strength, and with all your mind; and your neighbor as yourself." The attorney, attempting to justify himself and still attempting to test Jesus asks in verse 29, "And who is my neighbor?"

Jesus answers him with this parable about a brutal robbery. He talks about a priest walking down the road, seeing this victimized man stripped, beaten, and half-dead. The priest walks on the other side of the road to avoid the wounded man. The Levite did the same. Both see the beaten man and walk away—both probably following Leviticus law justifying themselves by not touching a dead body—because the person was so severely beaten. Yet that same priest and Levite every morning of their adult life would say the *Great Shema* found in Deuteronomy 6:4-5: "Hear, O Israel: the Lord is our God, the Lord alone. You shall love the Lord your God with all your heart, and with all your soul, and with all your might. Hear O Israel, the Lord God is one." Every day that priest and Levite would say those words, yet both walked by. The Bible says in contrast to the two religious leaders, the Samaritan looked upon the man who was beaten, and he had *compassion* on him. He was *suffering with* him. The Samaritan took care of him by mending him, and providing the wounded man a place to stay at his own expense (see Luke 10:25-37).

The only other time this Greek word translated as "compassion" is used is in the parable of the Prodigal Son in Luke 15:11-32. The younger son apparently had such a disagreement with his father that he demanded his inheritance immediately. In essence the son was only thinking of himself. The Bible says he squandered all his money, so much so, that this Jewish boy ended up at a pig farm, which is not exactly the *kosher* thing to do. There he realizes, "What kind of life am I leading? I could work at my father's place and have a better life than I have now."

The Bible says that, when the son was walking toward his home, still thinking about all the things he wanted to apologize for, his father saw him from a distance. The father was filled with *compassion*. The father was "suffering with" his youngest son. When you suffer with someone, it always demands action. The father ran toward him, embraced him, and welcomed him back home with a celebration! You know the father had great compassion because the elder never runs toward the younger. Like the Samaritan toward the severely beaten man, and like Jesus toward the widow, the father had compassion toward his son—he *suffered with* him.

What God wants us to know is that—in the midst of our trials and tribulations, in the midst of our adversities and agonies, and in all the things we are going through in life—He has compassion for us! He *suffers with* us.

Many times in our healing ministry, especially in dealing with the healing of memories, we spend time praying for those who are hurting. We ask them to go back to the particular event that has caused so much pain. We ask them, in the midst of that painful memory, if Jesus was there. Many times, as they begin to examine those painful moments, they say, "Yes, I see Him." They see Him in tears. They see Him caring. They see Him loving. They see Him sad. They see Him with compassion.

I've been in ministry for a long time. In the pastorate, I've taught a great deal about the Holy Spirit. But in the first ten years of my ministry, I am sorry to say that I never fully felt God's love. I often felt like a second-class Christian, always thinking that God loved others more than me. I knew that God loved me, intellectually speaking; I just never felt it. As a result of never feeling His love, at times I wondered if God even cared.

Then two individuals prayed for me in a special setting—for three solid days—and it was the first time in my entire life that I fully felt the love of God. God broke through, perhaps because I allowed him to. His love flooded in over me and through me. His compassion overcame all my obstacles, attachments, addictions, hurts, wounds, and fears. I've got to tell you, it is the most incredible feeling in the world to know you are loved—truly loved. God wants you to know that He loves you. Deeply. Intimately. He has *compassion* for you!

When you suffer, He suffers. But there's more. It wouldn't be enough to know that we have a God who is passionate for us, who suffers with us, unless we also have a God who is the God of life and death. A Father who, when moved by compassion for His child, has the power to take action on our behalf. Just like the Samaritan for the beaten man. Just like the father for his wayward son. Just like Jesus for a grieving widow.

God Has Power over Life and Death

The Bible says that, when Jesus saw the grief-stricken widow, he had compassion for her. He said to her, "Do not weep." It was not just an American phrase to "Cheer up!" The Lord was being tender, very gentle. Luke 7:14 says that He came forward and touched the open coffin. The burier and the other witnesses must have stood still in shock. After all, what Jesus did was a violation of the ceremonial law. But Jesus knew the heart of His Father revealed in Hosea 6:6, which says, "For I desire steadfast love and not sacrifice, the knowledge of God rather than burnt offerings." Jesus said to the corpse in Luke 7:14, "Young man, I say to you, rise!" The dead man sat up and began to speak, and Jesus gave him to his mother. I love that phrase in the next verse, *"Jesus gave him to his mother."* That exact phrase is used in 1 Kings 17:23 in the story of Elijah ministering to another widow whose son had died. Elijah prayed and laid himself upon that child, and God raised that child.

God wants you to know that He has compassion for you. And God wants you to know that He has power over life and death. He doesn't just want us to have an abundant *after*life. When He speaks of eternal life, He is not just speaking of when you die. He is speaking about right now—that you may have heaven on earth. Jesus said, "I came that they may have life, and have it abundantly" (John 10:10). And, He means right now because God is a God of life and death, and of power.

Two Final Applications to Encourage Us

Because God understands us completely,
know that we are understood fully in the dark times and good times.

Nearly all of my life I have been looking for others to understand me. I wanted parents to understand the difficulty of growing up. I wanted friends to understand the challenges I faced in society. I wanted professors to understand how hard I was working to balance my life and school. I wanted my parishioners to understand how much I cared for them. I wanted the church to understand how much I was truly hurting when my son died, even though I knew he was in the arms of Jesus.

There is no one in the world who understands me more than my wife Bobbi. She understands my conflicting ways, my inconsistent methods, and my genuine heart for others. But even Bobbi, after all our years together, falls short of my Father God, who understands me without fail. God has compassion and suffers with me when I am suffering and hurting.

To be understood is one of the greatest feelings in the world. When someone knows your fears, your doubts, your dreams, your struggles, and your strengths—and loves and completely accepts you just as you are—your entire journey walking with Jesus in the holy life is a freeing experience! Don't just take my word for it; let the words of God soak in.

The annual celebration of Father's Day can be a difficult time for some people. For some it is a time of great rejoicing. For others it is a time of great pain. Did you know that on Mother's Day, prisoners send more cards out than any other day? Do you know what holiday they send the least amount of cards? You guessed it, Father's Day.

Many of you have had absent fathers, or if they were not absent, perhaps many of you have had painful memories of your fathers. I know many of them were simply trying their best but fell very short of what you needed from them in order to feel loved and safe in this world. If that is true for you, in all likelihood, you need healing for your image of God. It is difficult to lead a life of holiness, love, and compassion if your image of God is not one of holiness, love, and compassion. If we couldn't trust our father that we see, then how can we trust God who no one sees?

Jesus wants us to know that we have a God who suffers with us. He is compassionate toward us, as we seek to navigate the various aspects of our lives in good times and bad. Jesus always wants you to know that our God is always good.

*Because God has power over life and death,
we can live our lives with gratitude.*

Knowing we are understood is important because we know with certainty that we are valued and our life has significance. But there is one more application that God desires for us to know in this passage. Because God has power over life and death, we can live our lives with gratitude. Wherever you are in life, He knows it. He has compassion for you, and He is the Lord of life and the Lord of death. There is no need to have fear about this life or the next. Jesus is the Lord of life and overcomes the power of death. We can live our life just like Paul mentions to the church of Thessalonica: "give thanks in all circumstances; for this is the will of God in Christ Jesus concerning you" (1 Thessalonians 5:18).

Conclusion

It would feel unnatural for me not to miss Dallas Willard. He meant so much to me during my journey with Jesus Christ. God used Him in deep and profound ways in my life and provided a model for me on how to be holy, loving, and compassionate like Christ. I know that my Father sees my pain. He understands my grief. And He is moved with compassion for me. He *suffers with* me. And that gives me a depth of comfort in my loss that I would otherwise be missing.

I am told that the last two words Dallas Willard ever spoke as he moved from this life to the next was, "Thank you."

There was much talk among us who knew him on what that meant. Maybe Dallas just wanted to say thank you to his wife, Jane, and to his family who were there during his last moments. Maybe it was something else. And then I suggested this crazy thought that maybe Dallas saw Jesus standing up and applauding his faithful journey walking with God while inspiring us, equipping us, and encouraging us on this earth. Maybe God said to him, just the way a loving father would say, "Well done, good and faithful servant."

Dallas simply replied in his humble way, "Thank you."

Sermon 5

The Philippian Hymn: Ode to the Servant

Russell Duke

Philippians 2:5-11

Our hymns play an emotional role in worship as we collectively lift voices in song to express our response to God and his love. We see this same worship in song in the early church. Christian hymns were integrated in the New Testament text, adding insight into the beliefs of Christian leaders in the first century. A common query becomes a catalyst for reflection, as reflected by Charles Wesley, who penned his awe with this lyric: "How can it be that my God would die for me?"

The First Century Hymn

In the first century, the new Christians raised their voices in song to worship God. The apostle Paul called Christians to be filled with the Spirit, conversing with one another in psalms, hymns, and spiritual songs, singing and making melody in their hearts to the Lord, always expressing their thanks for everything to God, in the name of Jesus Christ (Ephesians 5:18-20).

Psalms were written by many servants of God, with King David being a leading musician and composer among them. In Solomon's time, choirs intoned praises of God standing on the Temple steps. In time, messages from God to his servants became popularized in song. One such popular hymn flows from the blessing that Aaron the High Priest and his sons spoke to Israel on behalf of God: "The Lord bless you and keep you; the Lord make his face to shine upon you, and be gracious to you; the Lord lift up his countenance upon you, and give you peace" (Numbers 6:24-26, NRSV).

Jesus sang a hymn with the disciples at the conclusion of his farewell discourse the eve of his crucifixion (Matthew 26:30). What an expression of faith in the face of impending trials that must have been!

In the city of Philippi, Paul and Silas were imprisoned for preaching the gospel of Jesus Christ. About midnight, they raised their voices in prayer and sang hymns of praise to God, undaunted by their prison confinement (Acts 16:25).

The Christian church has sung hymns for many reasons: "The distinctive Christian hymn was born out of a need to assert: (1) the centrality of Christ in God's saving plan and his unique relationship to God; (2) the true meaning of the Christian life as one of moral excellence; and (3) the freedom of believers from all forms of bad religion and superstition which would hold them prey to fears and doubts" (Gerald Hawthorne, et al., *Dictionary of Paul and His Letters*).

In song, Christians expressed belief in God whose nature as a loving Father is revealed in Jesus Christ. They often focused on God's saving acts in history.

The apostle Paul incorporates portions of many hymns into his epistles. The book of Ephesians contains a meditative hymn of faith in God's redemption (1:3-14) and hymns praising the rite of baptism (2:12-19; 5:14). Christological hymns praise God's action through Christ (Philippians 2:5-11; Col. 1:15-20; 1 Timothy 3:16). The Pastoral letters abound with hymns that confess God in Christ the Mediator (1 Timothy 1:15; 2:5-6; 3:16; 2 Timothy 1:9-10; 2:11-13; Titus 3:3-7) and hymns praising salvation in Christ (1 Timothy 6:11-12, 15-16). Central to Paul's relationship with Jesus is the Christological hymn in Philippians 2.

Historical Background to Philippians

Saul Paulus, a Pharisee of Pharisees, first understood God as one Being who created angels to do his bidding; furthermore, he would send the Messiah, a human being who would wear the mantle of authority and power of God. Saul denounced Christian heretics whose belief in Jesus Christ as Lord offended the Jewish concept of the one God, and endeavored to persecute them. He pursued Christians to Damascus to end their religious fanaticism.

Saul's mission, though, took an unexpected turn when Jesus knocked Saul—later renamed Paul—off his horse. For three days the blinded Paul considered his encounter with Jesus. Restoration of physical sight followed his spiritual enlightenment.

Now a follower of Jesus, Paul joined Barnabas to take the message of salvation to the Jews of the Diaspora (Acts 13:13-46). Paul told the Jews in Antioch of Pisidia that, since they had rejected the word of God, it was time for the apostles to turn to the Gentiles (13:47).

As Paul encountered the Gentile world, he was challenged to counter a wide belief in polytheism. In Athens, he was confronted with the Temple of Zeus, which was the largest temple ever built in Greece, including the Theater of Dionysus, the Parthenon, and the tiny Temple of Athena Nike. Paul was appalled, and "his spirit was provoked within him as he saw that the city was full of idols" (Acts 17:16).

Later, on Paul's third journey, he lived for almost three years in Ephesus, a city devoted to Artemas, goddess of fertility. Paul was forced out of Ephesus. So he continued west, through Philippi to Corinth, about A.D. 57, where he wrote to the Christians in Rome. By then, Paul had become somewhat comfortable with referring to Yahweh as God and as Christ. In Romans 9:27-29, the referent of the Yahweh text is God. In Romans 10:13, the referent is Christ, and in Romans 11:34, God again. He still believed in one God (3:30).

So we jump to the book of Philippians, written from Paul's first imprisonment in Rome, probably around A.D. 62. One of the themes in Philippians revolves around the Christian joy that saints experience in Christ, joy developed only through living the life of a servant. In Philippians 2, Paul appears to have interjected a Christian hymn, one probably familiar to his readers. He calls the church to unity, which is only achievable by following Jesus Christ, as Jesus is the true servant who cares for the needs of others.

The Hymn of the Servant: Philippians 2:5-11

Let the same mind be in you that was in Christ Jesus; (2:5)

To set up the hymn, Paul calls Christians to think as Jesus Christ did, to plan thoughtfully as he did, in caring for others, as seen in the Incarnation. They were to find encouragement in Jesus, consolation in love, and fellowship in the Spirit, humbly serving others as Jesus did.

who, though he was in the form of God, did not regard equality with God as something to be exploited, (2:6)

The hymn starts by using the present participle to describe his state of life as continuing and unalterable. The Greek word *morphēn* (form) generally refers to the form that most fully expresses the being, that is, its essential form which does not change. So the poem cautiously says Christ was by nature God, expressing it poetically. Christ was God in essence, immutable and unalterable.

The second phrase closely connects this phrase to the previous one; Christ, though God, did not think the nature of God was something to be "exploited" (NRSV), or "grasped" (NIV). This Greek word *harpagmos* is difficult to translate because it only occurs here in the Bible. In general Greek usage of the term means "to clutch" or "to grasp," and was commonly connected with robbery. A possible interpretation is that Christ did not clutch at his divinity, because he was God by very nature, not by choice or will. The NIV prefers the translation, "Who, being in very nature God, did not consider equality with God something to be grasped," while the NKJV states that he "did not consider it robbery to be equal with God." Surely there was no robbery or clutching at divinity, for Jesus Christ was by nature God as the Son of God.

So Jesus did not exploit his divinity. Paul's Greek audience lived in a culture that feared the gods as unpredictable and exploitive.

Zeus was the supreme, or high, god of the Greek culture. Proudly carrying a thunderbolt, he was the All-Father who was infamous for his promiscuous exploitation of goddesses and women. His most famous offspring came from his liaison with the mortal Alcmene, chosen by Zeus because of her beauty, virtue, and wisdom. Their son Hercules, as the myth goes, was noted for his mighty deeds, most of which were performed to expiate his sexual and murderous sins. The goddess Hera, the jealous wife of Zeus, sought to kill Hercules, but could not penetrate his brute power. Finally, on his funeral pyre, writhing in pain as flames reached him, Hercules was changed into a god in a flash of lightning and taken into Olympus.

Another son of Zeus by yet another consort was Dionysus, who was dismembered by a jealous Hera. He was resurrected by his grandmother Rhea and became known for debauchery and drunkenness.

Against this background of Greek mythology, the hymn assures Christians that God is acting from his divinity in a manner which is not exploitive of humans, in a way which does not clutch at his own power.

> *but emptied himself, taking the form of a slave,*
> *being born in human likeness. (2:7)*

This difficult passage provides the foundation for kenotic theology. The NIV says he "made himself nothing" (*kenōsis*), whereas the NKJV states he "made himself of no reputation." Taken in context, the hymn claims he "emptied" himself, while at the same time remaining God. The term *kenōsis* literally means "to empty"; thus, in poetic manner, this vivid term conveys the loving sacrifice of the Incarnation.

Within this hymn, what was emptied lies in the context of what was added, not specifically of anything being lost. God the Son emptied himself by taking on the essential nature of a human servant. The hymn claims the Incarnation was real, unlike the visits from the gods in Greek myth.

Jesus was born a human being. The aorist participle is used to stress beginning or becoming, a state which is not eternal, and stands in sharp contrast to the present participle *huparchōn* in verse 6, which connotes a continual state. Therefore one understands that the humanity of Jesus was real, but not always existing, for it started in the Incarnation. Therefore Christ always existed (*huparchōn*) "in the form of God," whereas here it is said that he came into existence (*genomenos*) "in the likeness of man" (Gerald Hawthorne, *Word Bible Commentary*).

The Son, being God, "made himself nothing, taking the very nature of a servant, being made in human likeness" (2:7, NIV). He took on human nature without necessarily losing his divine nature and attributes; he gave up the prerogatives of full sovereignty to become a servant, taking a new position.

Athanasius, writing *On the Incarnation*, summarized the existence of Jesus in the Son in this way: "At one and the same time—this is the wonder—as Man, He was living a human life, and as Word, He was sustaining the universe, and as Son, He was in constant union with the Father."

> *And being found in human form, he humbled himself and became obedient to the point of death- even death on a cross! (2:8)*

The form that Christ took on was humanity's "*schema*," a term which generally means "bearing, manner, deportment." This term usually refers to the outward appearance rather than necessarily the total inner essence. Christ became fully human, though not merely human. He took on the being of a man, one for all to recognize; he assumed through birth a form that would become altered with age and death.

Again, this hymn emphasizes that Christ truly became human. As truly man, Jesus Christ did not strive for human success and achievement, though in his sacrifice was the most successful of all humans, and did so for all humanity. He willfully humbled himself to serve us all, to fulfill the need for redemption from sin (Mark 10:45).

This humility included obedience to God. So not only was Christ sovereign in the sense of establishing law; now as the human Jesus he kept those same laws. This obedience took him to the most humiliating death, one reserved for slaves and criminals who rebelled against Roman rule, an ignominious death for Jews, for hanging on a tree or cross represented to them a curse from God (Deuteronomy 21:22,23; 1 Corinthians 1:23; Galatians 3:13; Hebrews 12:2).

The hymn poetically reaches the lowest point in the life of Jesus Christ, who being God, became human, lived as a servant, and died as a common criminal. His sacrifice was vicarious for all sin (Romans 3:23-25; 2 Corinthians 5:21). The crushing weight of sin was born by Christ. As he felt death coming, the man Jesus cried out to his Father in heaven the anguish felt from this estrangement that sin imposes upon humanity: "My God, my God, why have you forsaken me?" (Matthew 27:46). Jesus, though feeling the weight of sin's separation from God, also felt the closeness of God, for he also cried, "Father, forgive them, for they do not know what they do" (Luke 23:34).

> *Therefore God also highly exalted him and gave him*
> *the name that is above every name, (2:9)*

The mood of the hymn moves from the depths of the grave to exaltation in the highest place. Jesus Christ is again fully God, exalted from the Incarnation, now with a spiritual body. The hymn proclaims that he is "super-exalted." The Septuagint uses the term *huperupsōsen* for Yahweh as the one "exalted far above all other gods" (Psalms 97:9, Daniel 3:52, 54, 57-58). Here the aorist tense signifies singular action, which occurred through the ascension of Christ. This may refer to the public exaltation of Jesus, for just as he had been openly humiliated in crucifixion and death, now he openly has been exalted.

What is the name? According to the hymn, Jesus was given a name, in context probably "Lord," proclaiming his sovereignty.

> *that at the name of Jesus every knee should bend, in heaven and on earth*
> *and under the earth, and every tongue should confess that*
> *Jesus Christ is Lord, to the glory of God the Father (2:10-11).*

The hymn alludes to Isaiah 45:23, and implies that the honor due to Yahweh must now be given to Jesus (who is one distinction of Yahweh). The hymn calls for every tongue to confess Jesus is Lord, submitting to his sovereignty. "Paul is not setting Jesus up as a rival God or as someone who in any way detracts from the Father's special place, for it is all 'to the glory of God the Father'. There is no opposition and no rivalry, but a profound and perfect unity" (Leon Morris, *New Testament Theology*). Jesus is resurrected and given rule, incorporated fully into the Logos, one distinction of the one God.

Summary of Philippians 2

In summary, the hymn carried deep meaning for Christians of the first century. Jesus Christ, who was God, "emptied himself" of simple sovereignty by taking upon himself human life as a servant and dying a slave's death for humanity; his perfect humanity was exalted by God within the rulership of the Son, continuing to glorify God the Father.

Jesus had taught the disciples about his role as servant. "For even the Son of Man did not come to be served but to serve, and to give his life as a ransom for many" (Mark 10:45, NIV). Rather than the heroic warrior many Jews expected in the Messiah, Jesus was the Suffering Servant of Isaiah.

This great hymn in Philippians glorifies service and the Servant, in order to teach the inherent truth that service is followed by exaltation. Godly greatness is seen not in grasping onto power nor in exploiting it, for great love is heralded in service and humiliation. Jesus taught this message to the crowds: "The greatest among you will be your servant. All who exalt themselves will be humbled, and all who humble themselves will be exalted" (Matthew 23:11-12, NRSV).

Charles Wesley: "And Can It Be That I Should Gain"

Another great Christian hymn mirrors the love and gratitude of the Philippian hymn. John and Charles Wesley were devoted Anglicans, who both had ministered throughout their lives in dedication to Jesus Christ. John considered his experience in study of the book of Romans at a meeting in Aldersgate in May of 1738 as the point of assurance that the blood of Jesus covered his sins. Both John and Charles experienced wholeness in Christ, in fellowship with the Father through the Spirit. This experience in the love of God awed Charles, and he felt love and forgiveness as never before. Consider the praise of Charles Wesley with the setting of the Philippian hymn and his experience of wholeness as a backdrop to this great Christian hymn:

> Verse 1
> *And can it be that I should gain*
> *An interest in the Savior's blood*

Died He for me, who caused His pain
For me, who Him to death pursued?
Amazing love! How can it be
That Thou, my God, shouldst die for me?
Amazing love! How can it be
That Thou, my God, shouldst die for me?

Verse 2
He left His Father's throne above
So free, so infinite His grace
Emptied Himself of all but love
And bled for Adam's helpless race
'Tis mercy all, immense and free
For O my God, it found out me!
Amazing love! How can it be,
That Thou, my God, shouldst die for me?

Verse 3
Long my imprisoned spirit lay,
Fast bound in sin and nature's night
Thine eye diffused a quickening ray
I woke, the dungeon flamed with light
My chains fell off, my heart was free
I rose, went forth, and followed Thee
Amazing love! How can it be
That Thou, my God shouldst die for me?

Verse 4
No condemnation now I dread
Jesus, and all in Him, is mine
Alive in Him, my living Head
And clothed in righteousness divine
Bold I approach the eternal throne
And claim the crown, through Christ my own
Amazing love! How can it be
That Thou my God, shouldst die for me?

We praise God for his love and grace, thankful that the Incarnation continues in the ascension. The crucified, resurrected, and glorified Jesus stands as the representative and the substitute for humanity before the face of God. He draws all humanity to himself by the power of the Holy Spirit, having acted once and for all to reconcile humanity to God. In Christ, all human sin is forgiven and all humanity is loved and accepted by the Father. The Father eagerly desires that we be in communion with him, responding to Christ in belief and accepting the grace of God.

Sermon 6

The Trinitarian Life of Faith

[Preached on Trinity Sunday]

Brian Lugioyo

Romans 8:12-17

Happy Trinity Sunday! Today is a special day; it is particularly special because in churches around the globe more heresy will be preached than on any other Sunday in the church calendar. Preachers have spent the last week anxiously converting anything with a three-in-oneness quality into a witty illustration: Shampoo, conditioner, and hair gel trio pack at the grocery store; three leafed clover in the garden; appetizer, entre, and dessert special at Applebee's; all of these in the hands of eager pastors, with little thought, is transformed into the Trinity. In fact, rejecting the general three-in-oneness criteria, many years ago on this day I heard a homily in Scotland relating the Trinity to a six-pack of toilet paper, which the priest had purchased the week before. Incredible!

On Trinity Sunday the church affectionately dares to try and articulate the inner life of God as Father, Son, and Holy Spirit. And it is right that we do so, for this doctrine above all others is the foundation of our faith. The doctrine of the Trinity is the one key belief that sets us apart from our Jewish, Mormon, Jehovah's Witnesses, and Muslim brothers and sisters. And though this understanding of God is foundational and sets us apart from other traditions, we struggle to get a handle on it. Without much care preachers will fall into the temptation of trying to explain God mathematically with the general three-in-oneness criteria. And thus today God will become, across the globe, an equilateral triangle, an egg, water, steam, and ice. Or with orange in hand, the preacher will visually demonstrate how peel, flesh, and skin equal one orange. Ta-dah!

We contort our simple analogies and metaphors into impossible algebraic formulas. Though metaphors can be helpful, sometimes when applied to the Trinity they tend to be predominantly static, without life. But God is the most living being; God is dynamic; God is moving; God is here today; and we are, right now, worshiping this living God. Algebraic formulations will do us no good today; they will not bring us close to a living God.

Paul's Experience of God as Triune

So how do we begin to understand who this God is whom we call Father, Son, and Holy Spirit? Consider Romans 8:12-17:

> So then, brothers and sisters, we are debtors, not to the flesh, to live according to the flesh—for if you live according to the flesh, you will die; but if by the Spirit you put to death the deeds of the body, you will live. For all who are led by the Spirit of God are children of God. For you did not receive a spirit of slavery to fall back into fear, but you have received a spirit of adoption. When we cry, "Abba! Father!" it is that very Spirit bearing witness with our spirit that we are children of God, and if children, then heirs, heirs of God and joint heirs with Christ—if, in fact, we suffer with him so that we may also be glorified with him (NRSV).

The Word of the Lord!

What does Paul tell us here about God? No equilateral triangles, no peel, seed, and flesh of an orange, no three masks for an actor. In this passage Paul isn't describing God in the abstract; he is describing the God he has experienced. He is describing what the Trinitarian Christian life looks like. This life is a life in community directed to the Father, with the Son, empowered by the Spirit. Christianity is being part of a Trinitarian family. It is intimately entering into this holy and eternal relationship.

A Family Life *EMPOWERED BY* the Spirit

Let's look deeper at the text. Paul begins here with the words: "So then." This leads us to what was said before. In the first seven chapters, Paul deals with sin, death, and the law as used by sin. In the first seven chapters of Romans, Paul mentions the Spirit only five times. When he comes to the eighth chapter, where we find ourselves today, Paul uses the word "Spirit" twenty-one times. We're at a transition in his letter. Here Paul describes enthusiastically the Christian life, which is a holy life in the Spirit.

Verses one to eleven, which precede our passage, speak about freedom in Jesus Christ from sin and death and the indwelling of the Spirit in the lives of Christians. Thus, since we are beginning with verse twelve, we can paraphrase the "so then" as "if this is the case, that the spirit of the resurrected one dwells in you, then...."

If this is the case, then we are debtors, that is, we are under an obligation. Paul here uses this phrase to describe family life. Family life places us under an obligation. Fleshly life is its opposite; fleshly life—which tries to escape obligations on its route to becoming an autonomous individual—leads to death. But life in the Holy Spirit creates a new family. All of us here are bound to one another as brothers and sisters; we are God's family. We are brothers and sisters in whom the Holy Spirit dwells. This in part is the beauty of baptism. We are born again into a new family, and in this family there are real obligations.

To describe this debt incurred as the new family of God, Paul contrasts this new life in the Spirit with the old life of the flesh. To live according to the flesh is to live according to one's own self-interests, distanced and disconnected from others; living in the flesh is a desire to be an autonomous individual independent from God. Paul tells us that this lifestyle leads to death. However, true life is church-family life. That is, if the Holy Spirit dwells in us, then we are living true life in the family of God. We are "sons" (*huiothesia*) and "daughters" of God.

Living as a Co-heir *WITH* Jesus

God has a Son. His name is Jesus. And Paul knows that the Spirit we receive is not naked Spirit, but it is the Spirit of Jesus. That is to say we receive a spirit of sonship—of being children of God. Jesus, the Son of God, makes possible our sonship, that is, our adoption. Paul, here, highlights our connectedness to Jesus. We are co-heirs with Jesus; we are co-sufferers with Jesus, and we will be co-glorified with Jesus. Thus, we become children of God because we are attached to the Son; we are in Jesus. Put another way, we are the Body of Jesus Christ because the Holy Spirit places us in Jesus.

Jesus, through the Holy Spirit, enfolds us into His intimate relationship with the Father, with his "Abba." Paul tells us that crying out to God as "Abba" is the evidence of the Spirit dwelling in us. And thus it is the evidence of our adoption, our discipleship, and that we have been taught to pray by our older brother Jesus. It is Jesus who has taught us to pray to Abba, Father.

It sounds strange when my daughter Linden calls me Brian. It would be strange if I started calling my mom Liz. To call our parents by their first names is to begin to distance ourselves from them. Linden calling me papa and calling Nicole mama, this is the evidence of a close relationship, and being called papa and mama means everything to her and everything to us.

Praying *TO* 'Abba,' Father

Though calling God Father might be for us an old habit or even a struggle, its personal power must be recovered. Calling God Father is something Jesus does, and something only He can allow us also to do. The Hebrew Scriptures teach us to pray to *Elohim, Yahweh, El Shaddai, Adonai*, etc., and not to God as Father. Jesus, God the Son, brings us into His intimate relationship with God the Father. Jesus takes our hands and brings us into this relationship. He says, "I want you to meet someone; I want you to meet my Father." This is salvation. This is the gospel. We no longer are alone in the flesh fearing our dust bound return, but we are involved in an eternal and holy relationship. The Spirit of Jesus attaches us to Jesus; we are not alone, enslaved, or afraid.

But crying out "Abba" isn't always convenient. Eugene Peterson once said, "When we get involved with Jesus' prayers, we get involved with Jesus" (Peterson, "Regent Lecture on Prayer"). In the Garden of Gethsemane Jesus cried out, "Abba, Father, everything is possible for you. Take this cup from me. Yet not what I will, but what you will" (Mark 14:36). Here, in the gospel of Mark, is the only place where we have recorded Jesus' cry of "Abba." I think this is significant.

What does it mean for us to pray Jesus' blood-sweating prayer? In some way, getting enfolded into this Trinitarian relationship can be dangerous to our health. Praying "Abba, Father" with Jesus, if anything, should remind us that the Christian life is not mamsy-pamsy, but risky and often inconvenient. What we see in the gospels is that Jesus' prayers did not save him from inconvenience, suffering, or pain, but they plunged him further in the reality of salvation, which involved sacrifice. To pray "Abba, Father" is to dare to say, "I want in on this inconvenience too!"

N.T. Wright states that calling God "Father" is an act "of holy boldness. Saying 'our father' isn't just the boldness, the sheer cheek, of walking into the presence of the living and almighty God and saying 'Hi, Dad.' It is the boldness, the sheer total risk, of saying quietly 'Please may I, too, be considered an apprentice son.' It means signing on for the Kingdom of God" (Wright, *The Lord and His Prayer*).

The evidence of the Holy Spirit in our community is that we cry out "Abba, Father." It is what we do every Sunday in the Eucharist. We say yes to the broken body and spilt blood of Jesus. Eating and drinking, is crying out "Abba, Father"; it is an act that binds ourselves to the suffering Lord. Each Sunday in our eating and drinking, we pray together a bold and risky prayer with Jesus: "Abba Father, everything is possible for you. Take this cup from me. Yet not what I will, but what you will."

Conclusion

Thus the Trinitarian life of faith is not a life understanding an algebraic God. It is not static. Paul tells us that "through the Holy Spirit we've been invited into this most intimate and dynamic of all relationships.... We've been drawn by adoption into the loving embrace of the Trinity" (Samuel Wells, *Be Not Afraid*). The Christian life is participating together in the triune life of God. *The Spirit inspires the church to pray to our Abba with the Son. We are involved in a relationship directed toward the Father, with the Son, that is empowered by the Spirit.* God is personal, not a Trinitarian piece of fruit. Christian life is not about not-dying or about getting a ticket into heaven. Christian life is about living now in relationship with a dynamic and dangerous Triune God; it is life together directed to our Abba, with the Son, empowered by the Spirit— the Holy Trinity.

In the name of the Father, the Son, and Holy Spirit.

> *[Abba] Father,*
> *you sent your Word to bring us truth*
> *and your Spirit to make us holy.*
> *Through them we come to know the mystery of your life.*
> *Help us to worship you, one God in three Persons,*
> *by proclaiming and living our faith in you.*
> *We ask you this, Father, Son, and Holy Spirit,*
> *one God, true and living, for ever and ever.*

(Collect for Trinity Sunday, Liturgy of the Hours)

Part 3

Hope of Holiness

Sermon 7

Living the Reality of Death and Resurrection

Kent Walkemeyer

Colossians 3:1-4

An old comic book series based on the hero, Iron Man, was recently produced as a series of movies. Iron Man, the movie, introduces us to Tony Stark, a playboy billionaire genius who sets his life toward popularity, pleasure, and most of all profit, without regard for moral consequences. He does not care how his life affects others. He is singularly motivated by the pursuit of wealth, power, and fun.

But a near-death experience in a military zone transforms Tony Stark's life. An explosion peppers his body with lethal shrapnel. In a life-saving effort to keep the shrapnel from moving into his heart and killing him, a scientist plants a glowing electro-magnet into Tony's chest. (Remember, this is science fiction.) While keeping the shrapnel from moving into his heart, the electro-gadget inside him also becomes a powerful energy source. As a result of this inward life-source, Tony is changed outwardly. He becomes singularly focused on justice and righting the wrongs he previously caused. His new inward life-source also empowers him outwardly to rocket around in an iron suit saving the world, committed to new values, new actions, and a new way of life.

While the story of Iron Man is science fiction, the process of transformation reflected in this comic book movie helps us understand the process of transformation reflected in the New Testament. No, we do not get to rocket around in an iron suit saving the world. But through a type of death, and an implanting of a new inner life-source, we are empowered to live a transformed life. We are invited and empowered to new values, new attitudes, and new behaviors. For a moment, let us each consider the transformation efforts and possibilities of our own lives. How are we different than we used to be? What changes would we like to make in our lives into the future? How do we change? How does it really happen?

I have good news. Transformation is not science fiction. God offers us genuine hope and practical help for authentic transformation. It is not science fiction, but it is super-natural. By that, I mean we are not left to our own power or effort to change. God's grace provides what we need and empowers us to participate with God in the process of change. For example, look at Colossians 3:1-4.

The Scripture

> Since, then, you have been raised with Christ, set your hearts on things above, where Christ is, seated at the right hand of God. Set your minds on things above, not on earthly things. For you died, and your life is now hidden with Christ in God. When Christ, who is your [or "our"] life, appears, then you also will appear with him in glory (Colossians 3:1-4, NIV).

Like a reconnaissance plane attempting to get an accurate picture of a situation below, let us fly over this passage from different angles to get a clearer view. First, what does this text say about our past, our present, and our future?

Our Past: We died. We have been raised with Christ.
Our Present: Our life is *now* hidden with Christ. Christ *is* our life.
Our Future: We will appear with Christ in glory.

As a second flyover, what does this text say about our reality and our response? Our reality includes the truth about us. Our response includes what we do because of our reality.

Our Reality: We died and have been raised with Christ.
　　　　　　　Our present life is *now* hidden with Christ in God.
　　　　　　　Christ *is* our life.
　　　　　　　We will appear with Christ in glory.
Our Response: Set our hearts and minds on things above.

Let's follow this progression of 1) *our reality,* and 2) *our response* as a way of discovering how transformation happens. Something unique has happened to us. Something is presently unique about us. We can expect a unique future. Therefore we are invited to a unique perspective and response.

Our Reality: Dead but Alive

This language of being dead and raised to life is not our usual way of speaking. What does it mean? The writer states it as fact. Verse 3 says you died. Verse 1 says you have been raised. Earlier in this same letter to the Colossians, we find similar death and life language, not always with the same meaning. Death is sometimes used to describe the consequence of sin (2:13), but other expressions use death to describe what happens to us when we respond to Jesus Christ by faith (2:12). This latter use sheds light on our passage. In 2:12, the writer references baptism which represents death with Christ and being raised with him through faith. Colossians 1 expresses the same reality in words like "rescued from the dominion of darkness" and experiencing "redemption" and "forgiveness of sins" (1:13,14). Later in Colossians 1, we hear that we were formerly alienated from God but now reconciled to him (21,22). These are all different images of the same experience. Here in 3:1 and 3:3, the writer uses death and resurrection imagery to describe God's act of grace which begins our new life in him.

So we died. How can we understand that? To what did we die? If we invite our imaginations to return to the Iron Man story, like the self-absorbed Tony Stark, then we were born to a life pursuing all the wrong things. Romans 6:20 says we were born slaves to sin. We were self-reliant, rebellious, independent beings without connection to God or dependent upon God. Our thoughts, attitudes, desires, and actions all reflected this. But at some point, we encountered Jesus, and we died to that life. Not a physical death, and not necessarily a near-death experience, but God's grace released us from that life. Drawn by God's grace, we said "yes" to Jesus and "no" to the self-reliant, rebellious life, and this passage calls that a death and resurrection experience.

Using our imaginations again, and exploring another image from the world of science fiction, imagine each of us born with an electric power cord like the one on your electric trimmer or food processor or computer. We were born plugged into the wrong power source, a power source that empowers all the wrong parts of us. At some point, in a convergence of God's grace and our faith, that power cord is unplugged. That is the death of which our passage speaks. Then our power cord is plugged into God's power source. That is the new life. God's power now energizes us to live toward new values, new attitudes, and new behaviors. Other references in Scripture use the language of being brought to life spiritually (John 3:6) or of Christ taking up residence in us by the Holy Spirit (Colossians 1:27). We may not always feel this power or experience it fully in daily life. But it is our reality. We will consider shortly why we sometimes struggle to live this out daily. However, I want boldly to address a critical theological misunderstanding commonly held in popular Christian circles and some scholarly circles.

Our Reality: Hidden with Christ, Who Is Our Life

Hear this clearly! This act of God's grace leads to a genuine, substantive change in us that empowers us to begin living differently. God does not simply stamp "approved" or "forgiven" on us. He does so much more! Some Christians think and talk of themselves as merely "sinners saved by grace." This incomplete image projects a life that God views differently because of his grace but not experienced differently by us day to day. It is reflected in attitudes and language that view our lives as "always sinners, always struggling with sin."

I sometimes see bumper stickers that say, "Christians aren't perfect, just forgiven." Sorry if this offends you, but I dislike those clichés.

First, I dislike them because truth is too complex to be written on a bumper sticker. Short, pithy statements are always incomplete. (And I just gave you one!) Second, I dislike bumper sticker statements because they seldom invite conversation. They may provoke ideas, but it is rarely possible to engage in conversation on the freeway. Finally, and to my point, this particular bumper sticker communicates an incomplete vision of the Christian life. It communicates that the Christian life is not about change but about God stamping a "forgiven" label on an unchanged life. What an incomplete vision of the Christian life!

It is true that God's grace forgives our sins, and that is great news! It is also true that we will always be tempted to sin, always wrestle with the ways of sin in our lives and world, always experience resistance to the holy life, and will sin at times. However, the Bible now calls us holy people, not sinners. If we continually refer to ourselves as sinners, then we do not reflect what the Bible says is true about us. God has freed us from the power of sin and given us a new power source—His own Spirit. This is not a second chance or a new resolution, but a whole new life. This is not a coat of paint over an old piece of furniture, but a replacement of the old with the new. This is not an engine overhaul, but a brand new engine. This is not just CPR on our old hearts, but a heart transplant. God offers a death of the old and the resurrection of the new. Recognize the reality about the new you! You are not resigned to a life of sin that God simply overlooks because of his grace. No! His grace provides a way of escape from sin's slavery. You are hidden with Christ, who is your life! (3:3,4).

This image of being hidden with Jesus Christ, or the more common scriptural language of being "in Christ," reflects a profound understanding of the Christian life. Paul, the author of several of the New Testament letters, including Colossians, regularly uses this language. He chooses it as one of his favorite expressions of the new life: "If anyone is in Christ, the new creation has come: The old has gone, the new is here!" (2 Corinthians 5:17). To be in Christ refers, in part, to our core identity. Our lives have been given over to Christ. Christ is our life. We identify with Christ in his death, resurrection, and his present position of authority in heaven. In one place Paul says, "I have been crucified with Christ and I no longer live, but Christ lives in me. The life I now live in the body, I live by faith in the Son of God, who loved me and gave himself for me" (Galatians 2:20). In our particular Colossians context, the author wants to draw our imaginations into heaven, where Christ is seated in his place of authority at the right hand of God. He wants us to see ourselves there too, but not just in the future. Of course, we have a future hope of glory, which is clear from verse 4. But even in the present, our lives are secure and victorious in and with Christ as he is victorious. As some have said, Christ's resurrection brings God's future into our present. Today, at this very moment, we can experience a measure of God's future because our lives are hidden with Christ and, in fact, Christ is our very life.

So let's address the question that may trouble us most about this. Why do we continue to struggle with sin? If all this is true, if we are new creatures, if we have been freed from the power of sin, if God's Spirit lives in us, if we have died to the old life and been given a new super-natural power source, then why do our lives too often reflect old ways of sin? Why do we struggle to live our reality? The answer is complex. Life consists of patterns and habits: patterns of thinking and feeling, habits of reacting and behaving. These patterns and habits seldom change quickly or easily. Though God gives us the power to change and helps us change, forces set against God's ways have shaped and continue to shape our thoughts, feelings, attitudes, and behaviors. For example, our inherited depravity, our families of origin, our culture and its idols, and every experience of our lives has taught us self-reliance and independence. Transformation to a new way of living requires continual surrender to God, a continual attitude and act of the will directly opposing our human nature and all of the ways we have learned to survive in life. Like drowning swimmers whose instincts compel them to fight and struggle, when a lifeguard arrives, if they continue to fight, then they threaten the very source of their salvation. To survive, they need to relax into the arms of their rescuer.

A friend shared an unusual story about a man whose patterns of old, sinful thinking and behaving changed overnight. He was known in his workplace as an angry man, someone who would explode in anger and pick a fight at every opportunity. Someone coerced this man to hear a Christian evangelist. He reluctantly followed the prescribed pattern of response, not knowing how or wanting to pray, but mumbling something insincere to God. The next day at work, a situation arose that usually resulted in this man's explosion of anger. However, he responded completely out of character for him, demonstrating the fruit of a changed life. He had been changed overnight. We wish this type of transformation was normal for us, but it is the exception, not the norm. In most of our lives, this type of transformation takes time, discipline, and the help of other Christians. My own experience reflects what I believe is the norm. I look back ten or twenty years and recognize old patterns of arrogance and self-reliance have been changing. I see growth in my own attitude, for example, of a desire to be a God-pleaser rather than a people-pleaser. God and I still have work to do in me. But I thank God that he has brought some measure of transformation, albeit slowly. How does this happen? Our Colossians passage offers an insight into this process.

Our Response:
Setting our Hearts and Minds on Things Above

Once we comprehend and accept who we are as new creatures in Jesus Christ, then we can better understand our logical response. How do we cooperate with God to live this holy life? How do we surrender to the work of God's Spirit so that our lives reflect what God says is true of us as his people? If God views us now as holy, and calls us to holy living, then how do we live as holy people? What is our response to the reality about us?

Understand that most of the Bible is written to help us with this. Much of scripture offers practical guidance for living holy lives, or demonstrates how others before us have succeeded or failed at this. This particular passage does not contain the only lesson, but it does help. The author writes that the Colossians—and we—are to set our minds and hearts on things above. What does that mean? Are we to sit around meditating on pearly gates and streets of gold? Contemplating angels and celestial thrones? Heavens no!

In context, setting our hearts and minds on things above means that we move our attention away from the things below, the things of earth, identified in the next sentences: sexual immorality, impurity, lust, evil desires and greed (verse 5), anger, rage, malice, slander, filthy language, lying (verses 8,9). It means that we reorient our lives around Jesus Christ and his priorities. We concern ourselves with the things that concern Christ: love, truth, joy, holiness, peace, justice, hope, and so on (see verses 12-17). We attend to the issues to which Christ attends. Remember Christ is our life. We are in him. He draws our hearts and minds away from the lower, earthly things that distract us from him and keep us from holiness. He invites our focus upward, heavenward, to attend to Christ, to Christ's concerns for the world, and to our own personal and social holiness.

Hearts and minds set on things above? Once again, this sounds good, but how do we make it practical? It helps to consider the subtle differences between our mind and heart. Our mind is what we know and think about. Our heart, in this context, is what we love and seek. They are very closely connected, and each affects the other. In Christian teaching today, we tend to focus a lot on our minds, what we know. We work to educate ourselves in right beliefs, hoping that we will be transformed by the renewing of our minds (Romans 12:2). However, I have been challenged by the thoughts of James K.A. Smith, from his book, *Desiring the Kingdom,* to consider that our identity is shaped as much or more by what we love than what we know. In short, we are what we love! Smith says, "Being a disciple of Jesus is not primarily a matter of getting the right ideas and doctrines and beliefs into your head...rather it's a matter of being the kind of person who loves rightly." Think about it. Doesn't this idea agree with Jesus' emphasis on love? Smith goes on to say that the transformation of our lives results not so much from getting the right ideas into our minds—though this is a part of it—but from establishing patterns, rhythms, habits, practices that direct our love. As a simplistic example, if I establish a daily pattern of reading the sports page, then I will become a lover of sports. If I regularly and generously attend to my friends or family members, then my love for them will grow. If I wash and detail my car every week, then my love for owning and driving it will grow. If I daily direct my attention to God and God's ideas, then my love for God and God's ways will grow. Life works this way. What I regularly practice and give attention to shapes me as much as what I say I believe.

The helpful questions to ask ourselves, then, include: What do I spend time thinking about? Upon whom or what are my affections set? When my attention drifts, where does it go? When I cannot sleep, what excites or worries my heart? How do my routines demonstrate my affections? Honest answers to questions like these can reveal the direction of our hearts and minds. At the risk of oversimplifying the process, consider these three practical exercises.

First, identify and understand the ways our minds and hearts have been set on earthly things, the ways we have conformed to the patterns of this world (Romans 12:2). This is a lifelong process and a constant prayer for help. It is the prayer, "Search me, O God" (Psalm 139:23). It requires study of God's Word, attention to God's Spirit, and submission to God's people. Most of all, it requires a humble, submissive heart. We must recognize that almost everything else in our world draws our attention away from God and to earthly things like power, prestige, possessions, and pleasure.

Second, reset our attention. Grow in our understanding of the things above, things God cares about, like lost and hopeless people, peace and justice on earth, and so on. We let God's Word, God's Spirit, and God's people help us better comprehend what God loves.

Third, we reorient our whole lives around our new reality. Remembering that life consists of patterns and habits, we replace old patterns and habits with new ones, with the help of God's Spirit and God's people. Our values, thoughts, attitudes, and actions begin to take the shape of the new reality within us, formed by the things God loves. Our life is in constant renewal, like the process of shedding dead skin cells and growing new ones. We constantly shed our old ways and put on new ways. The rest of Colossians describes this process.

Conclusion

At the end of the first Iron Man movie, Tony Stark does something uncharacteristic of most comic book super-heroes. In fact, I don't think this scene exists in the actual comic book series. Super-heroes normally work hard to disguise their true identities. But at the end of the movie, Tony Stark stands before reporters, cameras, and the world to boldly declare his identity, "I am Iron Man." He embraced his reality.

My invitation for us is to embrace our reality. Before an audience of two, God and ourselves, let us accept who we are in Jesus Christ and begin to live out this reality every day. This is not science fiction. We do not get to wear an iron suit or rocket around saving the world. Our inner life-source does not glow brightly from our chest, as helpful as that might be. The transformation we find described in Scripture is not reserved for super heroes. Transformation is possible as we respond to our reality. We walk the world daily as new people animated by a new life-source. It is the experience of Christ-followers past and present. Surrendered to God's grace, we form new values, new allegiances, new attitudes and behavior. Our primary identity is now Jesus Christ, and we do everything in his power as his representative, living the reality of God's future today. Death and resurrection define and direct us: Christ's death and resurrection followed by our own. In this reality, we experience the power to live a new life.

Sermon 8

Esther's Banquet of Hope

Karen Strand Winslow

Isaiah 40.28-31

For nearly a decade, we have become accustomed to hearing about hope. In 2008, the elected "Homecoming royalty" at a sister university to Azusa Pacific University were called "students of hope" instead of queen and king. But hope is not a trend or relevant for some times and not others. God's people are always people of hope. Our hope is in God who demonstrates love and provides for us. Our God is here in us, among us, and will always be with us. God is for us, working on our behalf, strengthening us.

We hope in God, and God hopes in us. I recognize the hope of God the longer I teach the Bible and reflect long and carefully on each story and passage. God hopes in God's people, and God gives people hope. Isaiah 40.28-31 is one of the many Scriptures that conveys such hope:

> Have you not known? Have you not heard?
> The Lord is the everlasting God,
> The Creator of the ends of the earth.
> He does not faint or grow weary;
> His understanding is unsearchable.
> He gives power to the faint,
> And strengthens the powerless.

> Even youths will faint and be weary,
> And the young will fall exhausted;
> But those who wait for the Lord shall renew their strength,
> They shall mount up with wings like eagles,
> They shall run and not be weary,
> They shall walk and not faint (NRSV).

Isaiah declares that God is creator of everything, which is why we can hope in the strength God offers. "The Lord is the everlasting God, the Creator of the ends of the earth."

The Jews in exile from their homeland, living in Babylon in the sixth century B.C. (the historical context for this passage) needed hope to replace their despair over the great losses they had suffered. They questioned how these disasters could happen to them. They wondered if their god, YHWH, was weaker than the Babylonian god, Marduk. Why? Because Babylon had destroyed Jerusalem, burned its temple, and taken its king and priests captive, while killing others in the royal family and carrying off many Judahites into exile in Babylon. Babylon had defeated them in the name, and, so they thought, with the power of Marduk.

If the surviving, exiled Jews rejected the idea that Marduk was stronger than YHWH, then they wondered if YHWH had forsaken them. They had good reason to worry. Israel and Judah had repeatedly broken the covenant they had made with YHWH. The pre-exilic prophets had assured them that unless they repented, they would suffer the consequences, conveying God's anguish, distress, and disappointment over the people's oppression of the poor, their greed, their breaking the Sabbath, their idolatry and apostasy. The prophetic oracles are saturated with images of God's broken heart, and threats to deter Israel and Judah from remaining in their sin. Thus, Jews in Babylon were concerned that God had spewed them out of their land for good. They needed the hope offered in this passage from Isaiah

Later in the sixth and fifth centuries B.C., when the Persians conquered Babylon and helped some Jews to return to the homeland of their parents and grandparents, other Jews were scattered over the face of the Persian Empire, and many in Susa, the capital. They also needed reminders to hope in God. They transmitted traditions that have become part of our Scriptures, which nurture us with hope. The Scriptures, as well as our own journals and memories about God's words and work, give us the strength to survive our many ordinary days and occasional extraordinary days.

The book of Esther describes, not every-day life, but the extraordinary ordeals of two Jews in the Persian Empire. The courage and loyalty of both Esther and Mordecai are examples of how unusual, enigmatic circumstances can be used to turn evil into good when ordinary people are called to step forward for such a time as this: to be proactive, to take heart, and to take chances. Like other saviors in the Old Testament (Tamar, Joseph, Zipporah, Rahab, and Ruth to name a few), Esther took courage and used her wits to preserve life.

Story of Esther

Those of us who have heard the story of Esther throughout childhood, revel in how this young woman, occupying the right place at the right time, enabled Jews of the Persian Empire to survive persecution. Nonetheless, the book of Esther has not been without its detractors. Both Jews and Christians questioned its place in the biblical canon, and some groups probably did not include it among their Scriptures. For example, no fragment of Esther exists among the Dead Sea Scrolls found near Qumran, although every other book from the Hebrew Bible is represented there. Esther is the only book in the Bible that does not explicitly mention God or praying, although fasting is an important precedent to Esther's appeal on the Jews' behalf to her husband, the Persian king.

In any case, the book of Esther is here and full of irony, twists and turns by which the humble are exalted and the proud are brought low—a common theme of the Bible. The songs of both Hannah and Mary celebrate this sort of reversal, but the book of Esther is more subtle, more satirical, more comical in the literary sense. It is a comedy because it ends happily for the protagonists.

Esther was an orphan girl living in exile in the Persian Empire who was catapulted to the position of queen, after an extremely extraordinary event. Queen Vashti, King Ahasuerus' wife, refused to go on display with the rest of the king's wealth during three elaborate royal banquets (1:1-2:4). The king's advisors feared they also would lose authority over their wives and demanded that she be deposed (1:13-21). Their paranoia is satirized, as we shall see, for both the king and his main advisor, Haman, follow the advice of their wives throughout the story.

The removal of Queen Vashti led to a hands-on beauty contest that Esther won (2:1-18). She became the new queen, but kept hidden her Jewish identity (2:19). These violations of Jewish customs are bewildering even though they work out well for the Jews. Would anyone familiar with Jewish traditions expect a young Jewish girl to candidate to be the wife of a Gentile by spending the night with him? Or to hide her Jewish identity on order of her male guardian? And then acclaim her for doing so?

Nonetheless, Esther's story is hardly different from many others in the Scriptures: unexpected, unusual means bring desired ends. The Bible and church history are redolent with unorthodox means of salvation and preservation. Tamar pretended to be a prostitute in order to conceive a child by her father-in-law, Judah (Genesis 38); Joseph enslaved the Egyptians and obtained all their land for the Pharaoh to save them from famine (Genesis 37-50); the Midianite Zipporah hastily performed a circumcision to save her husband's life (Exodus 4); Rahab made a deal with Israel's spies visiting her brothel to save her family (Joshua 2); a perfumed Ruth approached Boaz on orders from her Jewish mother-in-law in the middle of the night when he was full and content in order to gain him as a husband (Ruth 3); Hannah promised to lend the son she hoped to conceive to the Lord, even though this meant giving him to a notorious priestly family (1 Samuel 1-2); Mary agreed to have a baby to be called the Son of God while still a virgin (Luke 1:6-38). Esther was taken into the king's harem, spent the night with him, married the Gentile ruler, and hid the fact that she was a Jew.

Even though Esther's story is no stranger than some other narratives in Scripture, we must admit, it is highly irregular. Let us return to it. After the king of Persia selected Esther to be his queen in place of Vashti, we learn that he celebrated his new wife with a banquet: "Esther's banquet." Soon after this, Esther and her guardian-cousin, Mordecai, who was always lurking about the court, saved the king's life. Mordecai went unnoticed, though the deed was duly recorded (2:19-21-23).

The Story of Mordecai

Although Mordecai was not rewarded, Haman the Agagite whom we meet in chapter three, was promoted by the king without explanation. The king commanded that everyone bow to Haman. When Mordecai refused, Haman decided to destroy, not only Mordecai, but all Jews. An extreme measure that required action on the part of Esther. Mordecai began a fast, taken up by all the Jews, gave a copy of the destruction edict to Esther, and told her to plead to the king on behalf of the Jews. Esther's reply indicated how dangerous this was:

> All the king's servants and the people of the king's provinces know that if any man or woman goes to the king inside the inner court without being called, there is but one law—all alike are to be put to death. Only if the king holds out the golden scepter to someone, may that person live. I myself have not been called to come in to the king for thirty days.

Mordecai sent his response:

> Do not think that in the king's palace you will escape any more than all the other Jews. For if you keep silence at such a time as this, relief and deliverance will rise for the Jews from another quarter, but you and your father's family will perish. Who knows? Perhaps you have come to royal dignity for just such a time as this.

As a result, Esther said:

> Go, gather all the Jews to be found in Susa, and hold a fast on my behalf, and neither eat nor drink for three days, night or day. I and my maids will also fast as you do. After that I will go to the king, though it is against the law; and if I perish, I perish.

Esther's Courage

Recall that during the first banquet at the beginning of the book, the king summoned Queen Vashti, but she courageously *refused* to come.

Now Esther, who was *not* called to the King, courageously came *on her own initiative*. Queen Vashti's courage set the stage for Esther to enter the story in order to preserve many people alive. Esther probably dressed as carefully for this interview as she was bedecked for her first encounter with the king. I will never forget the black and white picture that depicted this scene in the children's Bible my parents read us. Esther is in white robes, hovering in the dark hallway, hoping the king will hold out his scepter. As for the king, he sat on his great throne and fingered the scepter, leaving the viewer and Esther unsure whether he would raise it to her and invite her into his throne room.

As we continue to read the story, we find that King Ahasuerus did raise his scepter, at which time she invited him to a banquet. Just as the king had summoned Vashti to a banquet, now Esther summoned the king to a banquet, another feast we can call Esther's Banquet. She did not only invite the king, she invited the scoundrel Haman.

At the first banquet, she merely requested that the king and Haman return the next night to dine with her again. In between the Esther-sponsored banquets, however, Haman became further incensed by Mordecai. Mordecai's presence made bitter each of Haman's recent honors. His wife advised him to have huge gallows made for Mordecai. A tragedy of errors is developing for Haman.

That same night, when the king could not sleep, he read the records and was reminded that Mordecai had not been rewarded for saving his life. Just when the king wondered how he might honor Mordecai, Haman entered to tell the king about the gallows, obviously convinced that whatever he told the king to do, the king would do. Before he could speak, however, the king consulted Haman about how to honor someone with whom the king was pleased (6:1-6).

Haman, having become accustomed to honors from the king, thought the king meant to honor him. Haman proceeded to describe all the further acts of homage and tribute he sought for himself. Ironically, as the reader knows, this person was Mordecai, Haman's mortal enemy. Haman recommended that someone go before a lavishly crowned and robed Mordecai riding on a royal horse, proclaiming: "Thus it shall be done to the man the king delights to honor" (6: 7-11). The oblivious king selected Haman, and thus the latter was humiliated, shamed.

Haman rushed home to his wife with the shameful news, and she predicted his downfall, foreshadowing that very thing. Immediately, Haman was summoned to Esther's second banquet where she identified him to King Ahasuerus as the enemy of the Jews. She pled for her own life, which was wrapped up with the fate of her people, showing her solidarity with her kin. The king rushed to the garden in a rage. Meanwhile, Haman fell on Esther's couch—and Esther—to plead for his life. He gained speed in his plummet from honor to shame. In fact, when the king expressed his deluded view that Haman was assaulting Esther, "they covered Haman's face" (7:8). He was a dead man.

Conveniently, one of the eunuchs mentioned the gallows Haman had built for Mordecai, and the king immediately ordered Haman to be hung. Again, the great Persian king, ruler of an empire far larger than Assyria or Babylon maintained, comes across as easily enraged and susceptible to the suggestion of the queen's servants, basing a man's life—at least partially—on a misunderstanding. Clearly Mordecai and Haman are involved in comic/tragic reversals—one honored while the other is shamed, one lifted up to die, while the other is lifted up in honor (6: 7-11, 8:1-2, 7-15, 9:4). This pattern is found also in Joseph's story, in which the baker and the cupbearer's heads were both lifted up: one to be hung, one to return to the Pharaoh's favor (Genesis 40).

To resolve the edict initiated by Haman against the Jews, Ahasuerus allowed Mordecai to write another edict by which the Jews were allowed to defend themselves against anyone who sought to destroy them on the 13th of Adar (7:9-17). Many Gentiles stood with the Jews, and their attackers were slain over a two day period. This is the explanatory story behind the feast of Purim, a day of gladness and feasting for Jews to this day. The book of Esther ends with further exaltation of Mordecai, who received the wealth of Haman and became second only to the king himself. Remember Joseph, who rose from the pits of slavery and prison to be "father to Pharaoh," second only to the ruler of Egypt (Genesis 41-50)?

What We Learn from Esther

What have we learned through this dramatic Cinderella, good-guys-win, vengeful story? Certainly this story about an orphan and a king, feasts (ten banquets) and fasts, heroes and villains, sharp and dull wits, anger, courage, and composure is far more than a colorful explanation for an annual Jewish feast. But what *is* the message, and where is God?

As the book of Esther unfolds, it seems that God is thoroughly absent among these Persian Jews who had been transported from their land and never returned. They had no temple, no son of David on a throne, no prophet with oracles to reveal God's heart, no warriors or mighty men. God's promises are never mentioned; neither is hope. The denouement depended entirely on the wits and courage of a couple of well-placed Jews, with no explicit notice that God was with them as we heard God was with Joseph. Or did it?

The hiddenness of God is part of the theology of Esther. We recognize encouragement for Diaspora—scattered—Jews to be faithful to their people and recognize who is in a place to function as a savior. We realize that many times in our lives, we sense—no, we know—God is not here. We do not see God at work; we cannot find God or feel God's presence. The oppressors, our enemies, are getting the best of us. We languish like Joseph in the pits and prisons of despair, are under attack on all sides like David, or destined to destruction like Esther and Mordecai.

Looking at the book of Esther through the lens of Joseph's story provides insight to the hope and encouragement it offers to all of us who are alive today. Esther, like Joseph, was raised to a high position in order to preserve many people alive. She shrewdly retained the favor of a Gentile king, who had the power to save Jews when charmed and coerced. Joseph impressed the Egyptian king by interpreting his dreams—with God's help (Genesis 40:8), which delivered him from prison to the right hand of Pharaoh.

Similarly God was behind the scenes of Esther. Why would Mordecai refuse to bow to Haman, if he was not being loyal to God? Why would Mordecai, Esther, and the Jews fast if it was not to their God? By means of the dialogue in the book of Esther, just as in the Joseph story, we find its message for us. We learn that even against the most daunting odds, God's people are sustained, protected, and delivered. The story of Esther says that in spite of increasingly dark and disastrous circumstances, the unexpected can occur. Yes, "Stuff Happens." But, also, and this is the hope Esther provides, "Reversals Happen!"

Yes, there are problems with this tale that includes violence and vengeance that represents the vindication of the persecuted against oppressors. When storytellers develop powerful villains such as Haman as foils for lowly protagonists such as Esther, when each turn of the plot reveals the villains malice, those caught up in the story applaud the moment villains are humiliated. In reality, the Persians were not known to oppress Jews, but helped many return to their land and required them to set up their own constitution based on their traditions and history with God. However, the book of Esther, like the book of Daniel, submits that all was not well everywhere always, in spite of Persia's beneficent policies. Jews suffered discrimination and persecution.

Hope for Us Today

The book of Esther also shows that God still required human cooperation in the process of deliverance. God hoped in people just as they counted upon God. Esther risked her life in response to Mordecai's words: "And who knows whether you have not come to the kingdom for such a time as this?" She devised a plan to expose Haman's conspiracies. Esther provides hope for us today that is based upon cooperation between people and the hidden movements of God. The story of Esther says, with the help of those placed and called to step forward, deliverance is around the corner. Courage, wisdom, and shrewdness on our part, combined with proceedings only God can influence, lead to the salvation of the oppressed and the defeat of arrogant oppressors.

And this is our feast now, a great banquet of hope. Esther calls us to be pro-active for ourselves and our people, encouraging us to step out, hoping that the king will hold out the scepter. Esther shows the wisdom of moving forward in spite of the risk, and the danger in playing it safe. Esther says that when God is hidden and feels absent, God is working through circumstances that you cannot control. But if you had not done your part, then you would not see God's hand at all. Esther reminds us that the Lord is the everlasting God, the Creator of the ends of the earth. He does not faint or grow weary; his understanding is unsearchable. He gives power to the faint, and strengthens the powerless.

I will close with these words by Frederick Buechner that further encourage us to recognize how much God needs us to use what God has given us and the significance of where God has placed us:

> Hope stands up to its knees in the past and keeps its eyes on the future. There has never been a time past when God wasn't with us as the strength beyond our strength, the wisdom beyond our wisdom (*A Room Called Remember*).
>
> We have it in us to be Christs to each other and to God. We have it in us to work miracles of love and healing as well as to have them worked upon us. We have it in us to bless with him and forgive with him and heal with him; and once in a while to grieve with some measure of his grief at another's pain and to rejoice with some measure of his rejoicing at another's joy as if it were our own. And who knows but that in the end, by God's mercy... Christ's story will come true in us at last. In the meantime, this side of Paradise, it is our business to speak with our hearts and to bear witness to, and live out of, and live toward, and live by, the true world of Christ's holy story as it seeks to stammer itself forth through the holy stories of us all (*Listening to Your Life*, and *A Room Called Remember*).

Sermon 9

Who am I? Recovering Biblical Identity
Linda Pyun

Psalm 139:14

All of us are familiar with the story of "The Ugly Duckling," who struggled with his own identity until he found himself to be a beautiful swan. Yet so many people today, including Christians, still struggle with the same problem of low self-image, which hinders the formation of a healthy relationship with God and with others. Self-image has been treated as an important topic among sociologists and psychologists because of its close relation to inner well-being. However, self-image carries value beyond the realm of psychological well-being and into the important realm of spiritual well-being. Our self-image colors every relationship in our lives, including our relationship with God. If we cannot accept ourselves as we are, then how can we love others as they are? Moreover, if we cannot accept ourselves as we are, then we cannot believe that God accepts us as we are. Thus we must first value our *self* in order both to accept fully God's love and to love fully others as ourselves.

Types of Identity

There are two general categories for how we think about self. The first includes those who have a healthy (or accurate) self-image. They perceive themselves as uniquely created with unique gifts from God. The second category includes those who have an unhealthy (or inaccurate) self-image. They either float above the clouds believing themselves to be Cinderella-like people, or they suffer under a cloud perceiving themselves to be lower than worms (Psalm 22:6). What determines the type of identity one will form? According to Daniel Kim, the question of identity consists of three types: 1) Who do others say I am? 2) Who do I say I am? and 3) Who does God say I am? (Lecture, *Destiny Training Center*).

Sociologists say that human beings, even as infants, form their sense of self from the reflections and responses of others. Sociologist Gordon Marshall says, "Just like the reflections in a mirror, the self depends on the perceived responses of others." Later in our lives, our self-image is also influenced by our experiences—positive experiences may contribute to a positive self-image, while negative experiences may contribute to a negative self-image.

Recently TIME magazine commentator Joel Stein reported that narcissistic personality disorder is now nearly three times higher for people in their twenties as compared to people who are sixty-five or older. The narcissistic tendency of the *Millennials*—also known as the "Me generation"—is due in part to parents' desires to improve their children's chances of success by instilling self-esteem. Inadvertently, parents, in attempting to boost their children's self-esteem, make "an honest mistake" and accidentally boost narcissism. Because the Me Generation gets the message that "you are special" from a very early age, they later become disappointed when they realize that they are not as great as they thought. Regardless of how they feel about themselves ("I am special"), we cannot say that the Millennials always have a healthy self-image.

On the other hand, in ministry I see many people suffering from a low self-image, formed often by the influence of others. At a recent women's retreat, I met a pianist who came up to me after a session on biblical self-image with eyes full of tears. She shared her life-long struggle with low self-image due to her childhood nickname. Her grandma had jokingly given her the nickname "blue-melon," which signifies something that is different from the norm, since most melons in Korea are yellow. I do not believe her grandma called her a blue melon with any bad intention, but rather out of affection. However, as a young girl, her grandma's nickname led her to believe that she was different from the norm because she was ugly. As she grew older, these negative feelings about herself translated into low self-esteem.

Interestingly, some of the great leaders in the Bible used by God seemed to have a low self-image influenced by their perceptions of themselves. When God asked Moses to go to Pharaoh, his first response was: "Who am I that I should go to Pharaoh, and that I should bring the children of Israel out of Egypt?" (Exodus 3:11, *New Spirit Filled Bible*). Gideon also did not have confidence to be the tool to save the Israelites from the Midianites. He said to God, "O my Lord, how can I save Israel? Indeed my clan is the weakest in Manasseh, and I am the least in my father's house" (Judges 6:15). We also see Jeremiah excused himself when God called him. "Ah, Lord God! Behold, I cannot speak, for I am a youth" (Jeremiah 1:6). It seems that even these godly men were affected by perceptions of self that were inconsistent with God's perceptions of them and His plan for them.

Though our sense of being may be strongly affected by others, an identity defined by others or by ourselves may not be an accurate representation of who we truly are. True identity needs to be defined by who we are in Jesus Christ, not by how we are perceived by others, how we perceive ourselves, or by what we have achieved. If we know who we are in Christ, then our struggle to prove ourselves will be lessened. However, if we do not have a secure identity, then we tend to live life with all kinds of wrong motivations—to prove ourselves through performance, power, success, and so on. As Henri Nouwen says, when "we have come to believe in the voices that call us worthless and unlovable, then success, popularity and power are easily perceived as attractive solutions" (*Life of the Beloved*).

Christians' True Identity

So now let's focus on our true identity—what God says about us as Christians. There are so many Bible verses that describe who we are in

Jesus Christ, but I want to share critically important ways in which God views us that should shape how we view ourselves.

Most of all, the Bible defines our identity as beloved children of God. Our relationship with God as His children is the most foundational in Christian life. Just as Christ calls God His Father (Mark 14:36), the Spirit of His Son in our hearts entitles us also to call God our Father (Galatians 4:6). Romans says that we "received the Spirit of adoption by whom we cry out, 'Abba, Father'" (8:15). Being the Beloved constitutes the core truth of our existence (Nouwen). If we truly know that we are His beloved children, then there is no room for self-rejection from a low self-image, because self-rejection "contradicts the sacred voice that calls us 'Beloved'" (Dallas Willard, *Renovation of the Heart*).

A key verse that beautifully portrays us as beloved children of God is Zephaniah 3:17. In this verse, God's irresistible joy over us as His beloved children is very expressively described. After warning the people of impending judgment (Zephaniah 1:7,14, 15-16), Zephaniah counterbalances his message of doom with a message of hope and restoration, saying, "He will rejoice over you with gladness, He will quiet you in His love, He will rejoice over you with singing." Zephaniah describes God, in the midst of His people, rejoicing with gladness and singing over them. One of the several Hebrew words for "rejoice" used here is *sus*, describing a pervasive, irresistible joy (*New Spirit Filled Bible*). Imagine that the Lord's love for you is so deep that He is singing, shouting for joy, and probably dancing over you. I do not think we can altogether compare God's love to our love, but I imagine how most grandparents love their grandchildren so much that they almost spoil them. If you have grandchildren, then you may have a better understanding of God's irresistible joy over His children. As someone said, "If God had a refrigerator, its door would be filled with magnet pictures of us."

As His beloved children, we are precious to our Father. "Since you were precious in My sight, you have been honored, and I have loved you" (Isaiah 43:4). Isaiah 43 contains words of comfort and peace towards Judah after the message of judgment. God said the Israelites were precious in His sight in spite of their shortcomings. What is precious, invaluable to you? You may cherish your child, your spouse, or even your possessions. But we are so precious to God that He not only values us, He even honors us. If we believe that we are so loved by God, and if we really believe that we are so precious in His eyes as to be honored by him, then our identities should no longer depend on how others view us, but rather should be dictated by how God views us.

The parables in Luke 15 also give a glimpse of how precious we are in God's eyes. There is one lost sheep out of a hundred, a lost coin from amongst ten coins, and finally the prodigal son out of the two sons. Due to His love for an individual soul, God is more than willing to leave ninety-nine behind in order to search for just one who gets lost. The Bible does not tell us how one sheep got lost, but it seems obvious that it was not with the other sheep following the shepherd. In contrast, the Bible gives us detailed information about what the prodigal son did and how much the father was forgiving and accepting of him as he came back home against the cultural norms of the society. In both parables, there seems to be an intentional resistance to God's authority as a shepherd and a father. Nevertheless, our loving Father does not dismiss us for what we have done or how much we have strayed. Instead, he is willing to search for us in order to reconcile the broken relationship. Elizabeth Achtemeier describes God as, "A father holding a home-coming party for the son who was lost and found...[and] a shepherd exuberantly calling out to friends and neighbors that the sheep lost has been recovered." The parables deliver the image of God who is rejoicing over His people.

We, as His beloved children, are not only precious but also unique individuals whom God knew before He formed us in the womb (Jeremiah 1:5). As David says, each of us is "fearfully and wonderfully made" (Psalm 139:14). Ephesians 2:10 declares that we are His masterpiece, created to do good works according to His plan even before we were born (cf. Jeremiah 29:11). No one would call an invaluable object a masterpiece. Regardless of our feelings of inadequacy or worthlessness, we are flawless in His eyes. We are not unique only in the sense of calling, but we are also unique in terms of our story—our culture, background, education, gifts, personality, and spiritual journey. How we look to others does not matter to God because each of us is uniquely created to accomplish the goals that He has planned for us. I believe that God is writing a story for each of us using all of the experiences we have gone through and that we will go through. In spite of all the negative facets of our lives, God's good plan for us is bigger than our failures. And we know that the end of the story will be beautiful in His sovereign providence.

Changing Our Self-image

For some of us, despite our biblical knowledge that confirms us as His beloved children, precious and unique in His sight, we may still struggle with low self-image. A false self-image "can override everything else and cause us to act in ways contrary to all reality and good sense" (Willard). Thus, it becomes crucial that we correct our false self-image, and develop a solid biblical identity. But how do we do so? As mentioned previously, sociological and psychological approaches, upon realizing the importance of having a healthy self-image, have come up with many "how-to" models for creating and maintaining a new self-image. "Six weeks to a new self-image," according to Bobbe Sommer, defines a negative self-image as a bad habit and promises that it will take six weeks to break an old habit (*Psycho-cybernetics 2000*). The Mayo Clinic also provides four steps for a healthier self-esteem: 1) Identify troubling conditions or situations; 2) Become aware of thoughts and beliefs; 3) Challenge negative or inaccurate thinking; and 4) Adjust your thoughts and beliefs (Mayo Clinic, *Self-esteem: Four Steps to Feel Better about Yourself*).

However, changing our self-image does not depend on simply following "how to" guides to boosting self-esteem. Though suggestions from sociology and psychology may work to some degree, I believe that our most essential change comes from the Spirit through the renewal of the mind (Romans 12:2). In other words, our change of a false image can only come alongside spiritual formation as we submit ourselves to God. Our true knowledge of God secures our identity.

We can find a great example of how a person's relationship with God affects a person's self-image in Numbers 13-14. Among the twelve spies sent into Canaan, only Joshua and Caleb demonstrated an identity rooted in their knowledge of God. While Joshua and Caleb identified God's strength as their own, the remaining spies perceived themselves as mere grasshoppers (Numbers 13:33), threatened by the bigness of the Canaanites. This example in Numbers highlights the idea of thermostat vs. thermometer identity. Based on their knowledge of God, Caleb and Joshua demonstrated a thermostat identity—an identity that is set at a certain temperature and does not waver despite its surroundings. However, the other ten showed a thermometer identity—an identity that is formed by the environment. Just like a thermometer moves up and down according to its surrounding temperature, those with a thermometer identity allow their perceptions of themselves to wax and wane according to the perceptions of those around them.

As we desire to change our false self-images conditioned into being by the influence of others, it is important to remember that securing our identities as children of God is a formative process. Knowing God and knowing ourselves does not come instantaneously at the moment of being saved. As Augustine said, the Christian life is to know God and to know self. Just like our journey in Christ is an ongoing process of knowing who He is and who we are, our restoration of biblical identity will also be a process that takes time for us to embrace fully and live out the truth.

If we understand that correcting our false identity into a biblical identity comes with spiritual formation, then we will understand that the basis of a true self-identity is an intimate relationship with God. The long practiced and proven spiritual disciplines, such as solitude, silence, meditation, fasting, and worship will help us to be formed or reformed to be more like Him. These disciplines allow the Spirit to work in us and "they permit destructive feelings...to be perceived and dealt with for what they are"—our inaccurate self-image (Willard).

Importance of Christian Meditation

Among the many disciplines, I would suggest meditation upon the Word of God—the Bible—as our first foundation, since our thoughts must first be transformed in the process of recovering our true identity. Willard affirms that biblical thinking "undermines false or misleading ideas and images." He continues, saying, "Jesus loves me, this I know, for the Bible tells me so," is the main resource for correcting false and destructive ideas and images that control the life of those away from God. Interestingly, all of the four steps of the Mayo Clinic mentioned beforehand are related to the renovation of "thoughts," reinforcing the importance of thought processes in identity formation.

There are three levels of thinking: 1) information gathering, 2) conceptualization, and 3) meditation/reflection (Kim). Among the three, meditation is the deepest level of thinking and the most mature way of processing thoughts, ideas, and images. When we meditate, we need to pay attention to what we read, ruminating (chewing) over the Word again and again until we have "dialogue with the Spirit and with Christ, who presents Himself through the biblical text as the image of the Father" (Enzo Bianchi, *Praying the Word*). We do not just understand the concepts or meanings; rather, we absorb the deepest level of implication so that it affects our heart and soul. In this sense, meditation is helpful when we fight with negative thoughts about ourselves that are often subconscious.

I will share my personal story as an example of how meditation can change our thought processes. I recently had surgery to remove thyroid cancer. Although the most common type of thyroid cancer is not life threatening and promises a complete recovery, I was anxious about the surgery and the rare chance of losing my voice. A few days before the surgery, I was taking a walk toward the small hill behind my house, and meditated upon Psalm 8:4: "What is man that You are mindful of him, and the son of man that You visit him?" The Hebrew word used here to denote "man" (or "human") is *enosh*, meaning "to be frail, sick, weak, and sad." Among the four primary Hebrew words for man, *enosh* is man as a weak being, while *geber* describes man at the height of his manly power. The word "visit" is translated also as "give attention" or "care for" in other versions. Ruminating on this verse and learning about the nuances behind the words reminded me of the powerful truth that God is mindful of us because He knows that we are such weak, frail human beings who need His care and attention. In that moment of meditation, God addressed my worried thoughts, revealing to me that He is mindful of me in my weakness, thus dealing with the deep concerns inside of my heart.

Imagine that someone thinks of you (maybe all the time) and cares for you. If that someone is the mighty loving God who created the world and gave up His Son for you in order to redeem you, then what are you afraid of? Furthermore, think about God who pays constant attention to you and cares for you because He knows that you are such a weak human being. As we have more compassion for a child with special needs, God is mindful of us since He knows our smallness. That day, I came back home in peace, singing and praising the Lord and knowing that I am in His care. Our loving Father is truly concerned about our daily affairs. It is so true that "the center of divine revelation concerns man" (Juan Luis Segundo, *Our Idea of God*).

Therefore, one of the keys to embracing the truth about who we are is to turn to the Bible and meditate on its verses, as it contains enormous potential to change—by the grace of God—an incorrect self-image. Meditation leads us to surrender completely to the truth so that we are able to live out the truth. Since true knowledge serves to change our feelings and behaviors, we not only know but also absorb the truth that enables us to be free from a false self-image conditioned by other people and the environment. Through meditation, we allow the biblical truths to penetrate our lives. These truths will set us free from a false, inaccurate self-image that the world imposes on us without our consent. As the Psalmist says, the Word of God converts the soul, rejoices the heart, and enlightens the eyes (Psalm 19:7-8).

Conclusion

When we have a secure identity in God, we are able to rest in His bosom as a weaned child (Psalm 131:2). It is clear that Jesus Christ had his identity in relation to the Father as He said, "I know where I came from and where I am going" (John 8:14). When we realize we are beloved children of God, we have a true sense of esteem, worth, and significance. We also have perfect peace with ourselves knowing that we are in His unimaginable love.

Realizing our true identity in God and correcting a false self-image that the world imposed on us will not happen overnight. It is a process of replacing destructive, false images into a biblical image of self as a beloved child of God. As we realign ourselves to God through appropriate spiritual disciplines, we can conform to the powerful image of ourselves as God's beloved. Once we define our identities in Christ as beloved children of God, precious and unique in His sight, then we will no longer be moved by circumstances or by the evaluation of others. Instead, our confidence will bloom from a deeply rooted relationship with God, with continued meditation on the truth that He loves us, and that His is the best plan for our lives.

Part 4

Pursuit of Holiness

Sermon 10

On Becoming a Pearl Merchant And Learning to Please God

Roger White

Romans 12:1-2

For the individual who wants to live a holy life unto God and who looks to the Bible for guidance and encouragement on how to go about it, there is a very unhelpful directive found in one of Paul's letters. It reads: "Try to find out what is pleasing to the Lord" (Ephesians 5:10, NRSV).

Now a devout seeker stumbling onto this English translation will likely not find the language of this isolated text particularly instructive, supportive, or inspiring. If Paul knew what pleased the Lord, then why not simply say so, let everyone know, and be done with it? The phrase rendered "try to find out," sounds more like a polite suggestion than a serious command. Why not just unhesitatingly ask, "find out what pleases the Lord"? Adding the word *try* to the mix seems somehow to call into question the feasibility and viability of the whole endeavor. The reader is left with the vague sentiment, "make an attempt, put a little effort into it, give it a shot, have a go at it." For those in search of holiness, who are attuned to the accompanying divine quest, the language seems terribly anemic. The unintended take away message is: "good luck with that."

On the other hand, compare the success and immediacy conveyed in the following parable of Jesus, "The kingdom of heaven is like a merchant in search of fine pearls; on finding one pearl of great value, he went and sold all that he had and bought it" (Matthew 13:45-46). Here then is a simple, straightforward, successful quest story I suspect many fellow seekers will find appealing, motivational, and satisfying—search, find, acquire!

But we still need direction and instruction. How does one achieve the success celebrated in the pearl merchant parable in the midst of learning how to please God and live a holy life and not just end up *trying*? Since the message of Jesus' parable is primarily about the inestimable value of the kingdom of heaven rather than directions on how to please God, it is necessary to look elsewhere in the Scriptures for insights into that important quest.

Unfortunately, searching the Scriptures for answers can be just as daunting as pearl hunting. If I, with my unique set of limitations, am looking for help with how to live a holy life and please God, and on top of that, am looking to scriptures for answers, then how do I know where to begin looking in the Bible for such information? To what do I give special attention? It is like a map inside a map, a puzzle inside a puzzle, or to borrow a phrase from Winston Churchill, "a riddle, wrapped in a mystery, inside an enigma." We need help pealing back the layers to hear, understand, know, and live for God. To the biblical authors I want to ask, "Could you please show me where the pearls are kept?" And I want their answer to be an unambiguous "chapter: bottom shelf; verse: right in front of you."

In this sermon I propose three guidelines drawn from the book of Romans that are designed to encourage aspiring pearl hunters, those on their way to becoming full-time pearl merchants, and others wanting to learn how to please God in holiness. Romans provides a big picture and theological summary addressing how beliefs translate into practice, doctrines lead to morals, and faith necessitates faithfulness. The entire Roman treatise complements both the vision of Jesus Christ communicated throughout the Bible as well as the many images of holy living making up the Scripture narratives. From beginning to end, Romans is a well-reasoned argument on living "the obedience of faith" (Romans 1:5; 16:26).

Romans 12:1-2

About two thirds of the way through Romans there is a pivotal passage where theological exposition transitions into practical counsel. Future pearl merchants are encouraged to give close attention to how these verses bridge the book's two parts, provide an interpretive key for learning what pleases God, and extend an effectual hope concerning ongoing discovery. Chapter 12:1-2 reads:

> I appeal to you therefore, brothers and sisters, by the mercies of God, to present your bodies as a living sacrifice, holy and acceptable to God, which is your spiritual worship. Do not be conformed to this world, but be transformed by the renewing of your minds, so that you may discern what is the will of God—what is good and acceptable and perfect.

The first section of the book of Romans (chapters 1-11) provides an explanation of Jesus Christ's redemptive work, and from chapter 12 onward Paul urges believers to apply those truths to how they live. The first two verses of chapter 12 provide a foundational understanding, integrally connecting the preceding material with what follows.

Paul's appeal of these two key verses is personal and authoritative, much more so than was suggested by the directive mentioned above from Ephesians, "try to find out." Here Paul strongly urges and beseeches his readers. His exhortation comes at the end of eleven chapters of carefully developed argument on the redemption of humankind through the mercies of God, ideas succinctly summarized in Titus 3:4-5: "But when the goodness and loving kindness of God our Savior appeared, he saved us, not because of any works of righteousness that we had done, but according to his mercy." The weightiness of all the preceding material in Romans presses into these two transitional verses at the head of chapter 12, and the placement of the word *therefore* at this juncture of the text merits bold, underlined, capital letters. It shouts, "So this is how you are to live!"

The message of Romans 12:1 draws on a dramatic image from the sacrificial system of the Old Testament. Under the law, animals were individually slain and given up as an offering to God. However, now believers are to present themselves in similar fashion, not unto physical death, but by way of an ongoing consecration of one's self and actions, what Paul calls "a living sacrifice." Through the kind of personal and individual self-surrender Paul is advocating, believers become holy and wholly God's. One's entire being—physical, emotional, volitional, social—is included in this total spiritual immersion and dedication.

Ambitious pearl hunters seeking how to please God will note this first guideline drawn from verse one: *Be present to God continually*. In pearl merchant terms, "always be ready for acquiring new pearl inventory." Constant awareness of God's presence and an active turning of self to God is the essence of Old Testament wisdom—fear of the Lord is the beginning of knowledge and wisdom. Reverencing God in this way requires an ever-present vigilance, a praying without ceasing.

This all-inclusive commitment is made *in view* of the many mercies of God, not in order to earn them; the holy sacrifice of self is acceptable and pleasing to God based on what Jesus Christ has already accomplished. Elsewhere, Paul explains this comprehensive lifestyle practice: "No longer present your members to sin as instruments of wickedness, but present yourselves to God as those who have been brought from death to life, and present your members to God as instruments of righteousness" (Romans 6:13).

The figurative sacrificial language of Romans 12:1 points to and characterizes a spiritual and informed worship—one that exhibits active understanding—not the mindlessness and passivity of a sacrificed animal. Believers are to be engaged, intentional, and actively responsive to God. As Paul mentions earlier in Romans 2:4, "God's kindness is meant to lead you to repentance," and similarly here, the mercies of God are meant to lead to spiritual service and worship. They swing wide open the doors to living a life that pleases God and to finding the many pearls available along the way.

The next verse, Romans 12:2, addresses the mindfulness typifying those who want to please God. It yields our second and third guidelines, which are interrelated and complementary. The second is: *Avoid following the patterns of the world*. In pearl merchant vernacular one would say, "Never assume business as usual." The third is: *Align your thinking with God's*. Pearl Merchantry 101 would probably teach, "Think outside the box (or oyster shell)." Perhaps the J. B. Phillips paraphrase of verse two captures the combined concepts best, "Don't let the world around you squeeze you into its own mould, but let God re-mould your minds from within."

The World and God

What shapes and guides us? Verse two presupposes that two of the major influencers affecting us are the world and God. The proposed related guidelines derived from this verse reflect two sides of the same mindfulness coin: Beware of the norms of the world while adopting a God-referenced perspective; avoid one and align with the other. Our lives are characterized over time by either deference to a predominantly world-oriented way of life or to a God-oriented one. Paul urges the latter. This theme of the two ways is not new but pervades the Bible, and it is portrayed variously throughout:

- The way of faith and the way of pride
- The way of the wise and the way of the fool
- The way of the just and the way of the unjust
- The way of the righteous and the way of the wicked
- The way of life and the way of death

The emphasis is placed squarely on the antithetical nature of the two options and choosing rightly between them. Not surprisingly, the early Christians sometimes referred to themselves corporately simply as "the Way" (Acts 24:14, 22).

Does every person by nature (even fallen nature) recognize the oppositional dynamics of these two ways? I believe everyone has a sense of the tension; even street gangs and terrorist cells have some kind of code regarding "right and wrong"—however skewed in the eyes of others—by which they abide. Agreement on the particulars is certainly not universal, but the concept of the two ways is. Surely all people have some perception of truth, because everyone seems to know how to lie. C.S. Lewis in his classic work, *Mere Christianity*, begins with recognizing the two ways theme, and he titles the first section of his book, "Right and Wrong as a Clue to the Meaning of the Universe." Paul need not belabor the point. His readers, like us, do not need the idea of an internal moral compass explained; they (and we) need to learn how to use it again since the mechanism has been damaged, and the repaired instrument is still fragile from the restoration.

Distinguishing between the two ways in practice is difficult for us—a reality sympathetically acknowledged in the Scriptures—but the Bible never suggests that the choice does not matter or that there is ever an alternative third way that mediates between these ultimate concerns. The Bible does, however, promise grace, mercy, and hope for those developing a lifestyle exhibiting the dual guidelines mentioned earlier: *Avoid following the patterns of the world,* and *Align your thinking with God's.*

Furthermore, Paul's directions about the reality of the two ways do not require a person to see every detail of life in black and white terms, or to think continually in such absolute categories. Humans are too small and error-prone to manage this scale of living. Jesus identifies himself as the way to God (John 14:6), and following him in faith is our sole task, which is in line with the instruction of the first guideline—*Be present to God continually.* This attentiveness and constancy of faith, with attendant humble acknowledgement of the universe's fundamental moral dimension, allows us to move forward and collect the pearls that come across our path. The ultimate direction and goal of the search for holy living is not at issue, and once acknowledged provides the guiding reference point for following the lived details that emerge from the ongoing renewal of our mind.

How does this life of faith happen, and what does it look like? Followers of Jesus Christ are called to practice the art of discernment. In the individualistic and isolating times in which we live, there is help to be found in community. God never intended for us to figure everything out on our own. Regardless of where we begin our faith and new life journey, there are signposts of context and consensus pointing to Christ and to God-oriented living. The general revelation of God present in creation and evidenced in the history of the world, together with the Holy Spirit's superintending role over the church and the lives of the redeemed, point us beyond our limited understanding and outside ourselves. These influences help us resist being drawn into and duped by the worldly patterns we see around us and, through the witness of Scripture, provide models and motivation for pursuing the mind of God and seeing things from a divine perspective.

Christian literature across time, including the Bible, commentaries, biographies, and Christian classics, is full of accounts about the means and nature of the journey of faith, the holy life, and especially the maturing process of discernment referenced in these opening verses of Romans 12. The church's educational ministry has long had these major themes embedded in its curricular purposes and goals; Christian growth, faith development, discipleship, and spiritual formation have been its intended ends. Praying, serving others, worshiping, giving, receiving the Eucharist, proclaiming the gospel, helping the oppressed, and reading the Bible are some of the many ways Christian faith is expressed in community and are means through which growth and maturity are attained. But the personal challenge for each one of us still remains: How do we glean from the multitude of resources available through the church's broad ministry and apply them personally? How do I give adequate attention to the outward witnesses and internal convictions offering guidance to my life? How do I please God in my specific situation? How do I recognize the best pearls when I see them?

Applying the Three Guidelines

I conclude this sermon by highlighting a few suggestions for breathing life into and applying the three guidelines for pleasing God and holy living that we have drawn from Romans 12:1-2:

1. Be present to God continually.
2. Avoid following the patterns of the world.
3. Align your thinking with God's.

What follows are opportunity avenues that lead to maturity in discerning the will of God for one's daily actions and life. They will also help entrepreneurs in the pearl business.

First, follow the directions you have. In other words, recognize the pearls right in front of you. Heed the instruction and examples received from God, the church and Scripture, as you know them. Do not ignore the road signs that are already in place for your journey. This includes receiving counsel from others: friends, family, clergy, professionals, and those who have gone before us. Success requires a healthy self-awareness, the rooting out of blind spots, and acknowledging ever-present shortcomings and limitations. We all at times are easily deceived. With all humility we must begin by reflecting God's image and message in whatever we do, loving God and neighbor, and seeking first the reality of God's reign over all the earth.

Second, seek the welfare of God's creation. In other words, tend the pearls you have found and acquired. Steward the cultural, political, and geographic resources within your power for the good of all people. Help the poor, the weak, the hurting, and the marginalized. Care for the earth; it is God's property. While working on behalf of and seeking to advance the well being of the whole world and its inhabitants, simultaneously remain wary of the ways and patterns of the world with its too often shortsighted answers and illusion of expedited solutions. At the same time, do not neglect the creational norms and patterns of nature that are clues to how creation is fashioned and how it works. Jesus Christ has rescued us and "set us free from the present evil age" (Galatians 1:4), and we can be witnesses to this truth, proclaiming and applying the benefits of that redemption.

Third, and lastly, renew your mind continually. In other words, study the pearls you own and cultivate new strategies for acquiring more. The trajectory of our lives has been reversed from the darkened mind of Romans 1:21 to the renewed mind of Romans 12:2, but we must keep learning and growing in understanding. The mindfulness and discernment we are nurturing is not simply focused on the rationalistic aspects of the mind, but our heart and entire being: our emotions, imagination, body, and will. Submit to wise teachers to gain knowledge, read books (especially old ones) to secure perspective, and engage the mind's eye for seeing beyond yourself and our era into the depths of God, God's purposes, and the unlimited opportunities of grace-filled living. In so doing we will no longer be chronically seeking to please the world but will be developing the habit of pleasing God in all we do (including being pearl merchants).

By constantly applying the three proposed guidelines drawn from Romans 12:1-2, we may gain an increasing ability to discern the will of God—a way that is characterized by the good, acceptable, and perfect. The resulting lifestyle is opposite to the one referenced at the end of the book of Judges, where the people—lacking the God-orienting perspective provided by a divinely appointed king—simply "did what was right in their own eyes" (21:25). The discernment developed through following these guidelines also provides an antidote to the Proverb, "There is a way that seems right to a person, but its end is the way to death" (14:12). Paul holds out a greater promise in Romans—one that hopeful pearl merchants and those seeking to please God can readily embrace and follow.

>   1. *Be present to God continually.*
>   2. *Avoid following the patterns of the world.*
>   3. *Align your thinking with God's.*

Sermon 11

A Lesson from the Kernel

Daniel Newman

John 12:20-32

We have a squirrel that lives in the neighborhood, moving along fences and between trees. I find it not only entertaining but somehow calming to watch its antics. One of the squirrel's favorite behaviors seems to be that of burying acorns. It certainly expends much of its energy flitting around the yard, digging little holes, stuffing acorns into them, and covering them with soil. We know that squirrels do this every year to prepare for winter. One study found that they may recover as little as 26% of these for food. That leaves up to 74% unclaimed. What happens to these? What becomes of the acorns that the squirrel doesn't get back to?

We know the answer. They lay buried in the ground and die. But is that the end? No. In fact last spring I found two oak tree saplings growing in different areas of my yard. The acorns had sprouted back to life and are now on the path to becoming behemoths that could produce more than 5,000,000 acorns over their lifetime!

Jesus Christ employed a similar illustration before he went to the cross to explain what he was about to do. He said, "unless a kernel of wheat falls to the ground and dies, it remains only a single seed. But if it dies, it produces many seeds" (John 12:24, NIV).

We are called to follow Jesus with all of the ramifications that accompany such a commitment. So, what does this mean in the case of the kernel? What did it mean for Jesus? What does it mean for us? To this we now turn our attention.

Jesus' Path to Glory

We find in John 12:20-32 that Jesus has entered Jerusalem for his final Passover feast. In the midst of what must have been a feverish time, a group of Greek worshipers desires an audience with him. They seek out Philip (21). Perhaps it was on account of his Greek name, or possibly because he was from Bethsaida in Galilee of the Gentiles, and there was some type of familiarity. In any case, earlier in Jesus' ministry, Philip had brought Nathaniel, a Hebrew, to meet Jesus (John 1:44). Now we see him, along with Jesus' ministry, expanding their circles to engage non-Jewish people.

Upon meeting the Greeks Philip goes to find Andrew (John 12:22). Together with Philip, Andrew seems to have made it a personal habit to bring people to Jesus. Upon recognizing that Jesus was the long awaited Messiah, he immediately locates his brother, Simon Peter, and takes him to see Jesus (John 1:41-42). Whereas Philip didn't know what to do when Jesus tested him at the feeding of the five thousand and considered only financial costs (John 6:5-7), Andrew brought a little boy who had a small donation to make and set him before Jesus (John 6:8-9). Now, in cooperation, they bring this group of traditional outsiders to an encounter with the Lord.

Jesus has an interesting response to the news of these visitors. He says, "The hour has come for the Son of Man to be glorified" (John 12:23). What is going on? How will Jesus be glorified? He also says that the Father will be glorified (28). How will this happen? It would seem that the arrival of this company is a sign to Jesus that he is now moving beyond the prescribed limits of Jewish cultural boundary toward fulfilling his mission as "the Lamb of God, who takes away the sin of the world" (John 1:29). Jesus is about to declare that he will draw all people to himself (John 12:32). In this visitation we see that this work has already begun.

The Kernel

Jesus continues by presenting the image of a kernel of wheat (Luke 12:24). This is key to understanding how he, as well as the Father, will be glorified. I don't know whether to call it a path or a process, but we see here a pattern that the spiritual life demands of us, just as it did of Jesus. The kernel provides a lesson from natural revelation that Jesus calls us to consider. To accomplish that for which it was created, the kernel must submit to its Designer's plan.

First the kernel must fall to the ground. In a sense, Jesus had already initiated this process. We read in Philippians 2:6-7 that Jesus "did not consider equality with God something to be grasped, but made himself nothing, taking the very nature of a servant, being made in human likeness." Jesus, in some vital way, laid down his rights. He surrendered to the plans and purposes of God. He said to the Father, "not my will, but yours be done" (Luke 22:42). He humbled himself and became obedient (Philippians 2:8). In the incarnation he, the one who is the image of the invisible God (Colossians 1:15), the one in whom the fullness of God dwelt (Colossians 1:19), condescends to come and dwell among us (John 1:14). He, as the kernel, lays aside his glory and descends from heaven to earth. Can anyone imagine a greater falling to the ground than this?

Jesus further illustrates this principle just a short time later when he leads his disciples into the upper room for the last supper. We know the story well. Having walked the road to their destination and gathered in the room for the meal, they find themselves with dirty feet and no one to do the dirty job of washing them. How many awkward moments pass before Jesus takes the initiative I have often wondered. How uncomfortable were those sitting around the table? Yet no one budged. Jesus is their teacher and Lord (John 13:13). All things had been put under his power. He knew that he had come from and was returning to God (John 13:3). Given all of these facts, what does Jesus do? He physically demonstrates his emptying, falling to the ground, to his followers.

There seems to me significance to the order of what happens in John 13:4. First, Jesus gets up. There is deliberateness in what he is doing; it is very intentional. His emptying is not by accident. Next Jesus takes off his outer garment. Before he takes up the work of a servant he lets go of his status; he lays it down. The kernel falls to the ground again. Setting aside his position as their Lord, Jesus also relinquishes his right to be served. Rather than demanding that those present attend him, he releases them from their obligation to see to his needs. It is after this humbling that he takes up the attire of the servant. Having risen from the meal and removed his outer garment, Jesus then wraps the towel around his waist. He handed over his gown to receive a towel in its stead. Having made himself nothing, he takes up the very nature of a servant (Philippians 2:7). This is illustrative of the downward movement that we see in Jesus' life.

What next? The kernel must die. The message is clear. It can be neither missed nor avoided, and if it doesn't startle us, perhaps we are further from the kingdom than we wish to admit. In living his incarnation and mission, Jesus "became obedient to death—even death on a cross" (Philippians 2:8). His humiliation is followed by his crucifixion. The kernel must fall to the ground and die! A surrendering of his life is required, a complete obedience to God's will. Not only is there a letting go of rights; there is a release of the claim to life itself. We witness an utter submission to and reliance upon God, even though this path takes him to the cross and into the tomb. It requires a burial that blots out all light, all signs and symbols of life. In a sense there is an embrace of that which we would normally define as darkness in the process of his self-emptying.

The kernel of wheat must fall to the ground and die. If it does not go through this process, it is still very much a single seed (John 12:24). It is isolated, alone. Ah, but what of the kernel that acquiesces to the prescribed course? And what becomes of Jesus when he voluntarily lays down his life? Jesus said that the kernel of wheat that dies "produces many seeds" (24). There is actually great hope in the message of the kernel. Its death is not its end. Rather, death is its transformation! Jesus proclaimed, "But I, when I am lifted up from the earth, will draw all men to myself" (32). What a declaration of victory! His falling to the ground and death don't have the final word. We see this with great clarity as we remember what took place after Jesus entered the grave. Our celebration of worship each Sunday doesn't stop at the forgiveness offered in the cross, at Christ paying of our debt. The very day of our gathering recalls that he didn't stay dead, that the grave couldn't keep him. Like the kernel that springs back to life, Jesus rose from the ground that he had fallen to, and in so doing he reclaimed life as his domain and as that of his kingdom. This is the consummation of our joy and that in which we participate as we gather together each week.

And still there is more! As we recite in the Apostles' Creed, "he ascended into Heaven and sitteth on the right hand of God, the Father almighty." After his resurrection, after he took up life again, he ascended. He went to that place where all things were put under his feet (Ephesians 1:22). He took up his reign over creation. He accepted the authority of one on the throne as his enemies become a footstool for his feet (Luke 20:43). He assumed his glory once more. He who emptied himself was filled again. It was the lowest path that led to the greatest height. As we noted earlier, at the request of the Greek worshipers to meet with Jesus, he declared, "The hour has come for the Son of Man to be glorified" (John 12:23). Jesus rose again, ascended and received his glory. This all took place because he first fell to the ground, died and was buried.

Following Jesus

Do we think that this was a simple thing? Was it easy for Jesus to walk this route? Most assuredly not. He freely confessed before his disciples, "Now my heart is troubled" (John 12:27). We know that he prayed in the Garden of Gethsemane, "Father, if you are willing, take this cup from me" (Luke 22:42). Nonetheless, he submitted to and endured this way knowing that his surrender would become his triumph. He boldly declares, "now the prince of this world will be driven out" (John 12:31). Contrary to normal logic, this downward movement was his means to overcome the evil one. It was an apparent path of weakness that in reality was the way to strength. He further proclaims, "But I, when I am lifted up from the earth, will draw all men to myself" (32). God took Jesus through death to bring about the resurrection and life, not only for Jesus, but for all people.

So, how do we feel about life? Do we love our life? Do we cling tightly to it? Do we demand our rights and constantly seek to get our own way, to control our destiny and the roads we will travel? Jesus sharply stated that, "The man who loves his life will lose it" (John

12:25), and that the one who "serves me must follow me" (26). To follow Jesus means that we must embrace the path that he blazed before us. Like him, we must fall to the ground. Like him, we must go through an emptying. Like our Lord, we must surrender.

For us, as compared to Jesus, this is more a cyclical process. Just because we might have experienced something like this at some point in the past doesn't mean that we are finished. We all know by our own experience that spiritual growth is not linear. There are both successes and failures. It is not a straight line, not a constant progression. We often say, "Two steps forward, one step back." We are frequently faced with the need to relearn lessons from our past. There is a rhythm in our journey, cycles as it were. Yet, it is not genuinely cyclical either. A cycle simply repeats itself; it goes around in circles. To understand how we advance we need to overlay the cycle on the linear timeline. It becomes more like a spiral. We are making headway. There is a type of forward movement, a maturing process. Yet there are frequent repetitions and recurrences.

One of the points that we must consistently revisit on the spiral is that of emptying, of falling to the ground, of humbling ourselves. We get into so much trouble because we demand our rights. In modern society, if our rights are wronged, then we sue the offender. We want justice (as we perceive it should be). We want to vent our anger. We want to get our own way. We don't want to submit to the will of another. We want to do what we want to do. Jesus said, "The man who loves his life will lose it, while the man who hates his life in this world will keep it for eternal life" (25). Until we can learn to let go, until we can practice true surrender, we cannot experience the grander things God has in store for us.

Jesus went to the place of death. He fell to the ground and died. We must often return to that place, to the cross, recognizing it not only as the place of Christ's death, but of our own as well. With Paul we must learn to confess, "I have been crucified with Christ and I no longer live, but Christ lives in me" (Galatians 2:20). I say "we," but truly it is me. I must go to this place. How often my own will rises up in defiance and asserts its own importance. In contrast, Jesus freely surrendered to the will of the Father. He obeyed even to death. He relinquished his claim on life. He let go of power and privilege, comfort and convenience. He proceeded to the cross and the tomb. Will I follow even to, or especially to, this place? I must die that Christ may live in me.

We follow Jesus. This journey with him certainly begins in a downward motion. It requires an emptying, a dying, a passage into the grave. Yet as with Jesus, this is not its end. We pass through surrender to a newer, fuller, richer life. We, like the kernel, go through a transformation. In giving up our life we discover it in fullness. In the place of emptying, we are filled. Growth transpires, and many seeds are produced. It is to God's glory that we bear much fruit (John 15:8). If the beginning of the process is downward in direction, its conclusion is upward movement. The paradox of the gospel is revealed in us—treasure in earthen vessels.

Living in Jesus

We follow Jesus. Through his journey, Jesus overcame the prince of this world. Darkness was defeated; the Accuser was silenced; the grave lost its sting. For us, too, this is the way of liberation. Freedom from condemnation becomes our reality. As Jesus overcame the prince of this world, so we are released from the oppression of our failures and weaknesses. We begin to dwell in a realm where life and love reign. As Jesus' death produced life, so life in abundance begins to grow in us.

If we follow Jesus to the place of death, then we will find that in him we are not abandoned to the grave. Rather, "If we have been united with him like this in his death, we will certainly also be united with him in his resurrection. For we know that our old self was crucified with him so that the body of sin might be done away with, that we should no longer be slaves to sin" (Romans 6:5-6). In our union with Christ, the old is gone and the new has come. Fears lose their power; new life and its patterns begin to abide in us. We are transformed, renewed. This is our hope in the midst of tempest, turmoil, trouble, and toil. God has more in store!

Jesus ascended and is seated at the right hand of God. His enemies have become his footstool. Ephesians 2:6 tells us, "God raised us up with Christ and seated us with him in the heavenly realms in Christ Jesus." By following the pattern of the kernel, we are elevated to a place where the things that so concerned us in the past no longer have sway over us; they have lost their hold. A new perspective on life is ours. We begin now to see through the eyes of eternity. What seemed so important to us starts to fade as we enter the process of being formed after the image of Christ. We have gained eternal life (John 12:25), living in the knowledge and presence of God even now. Surely his kingdom is among us!

Conclusion

The kernel teaches us vital truths in following Jesus. To walk in his footsteps we must fall to the ground. In the process of humbly emptying ourselves we are called to give up our demands and our presumed rights. We must die, relinquishing the claims we place on our own life. Having entered the grave with Jesus, we likewise enter new life in him; we are raised in transformation. He lives in us, and our lives start bearing the fruit of that relationship. In being seated with him we become participants in and sharers of heaven on earth. The kernel is our teacher. May we learn and live the lesson well.

Sermon 12

It's Not Too Late to Be Holy

Sarah Sumner

"Be holy for I am holy," says the Lord
(I Peter 1:16, NASB).

To be holy means to be set apart. It means to be differentiated from the norm by making God, not anything else, your "reference point." Holiness requires us to let go of worldliness and embrace the hand of God—and walk by faith with God even into the valley of the shadow of death.

John Chambers was a man who knew holiness and unholiness. For lots of years he lived in debauchery and self-centeredness. John did unspeakable things at times, and he stayed hardened without remorse. But he was a mixed character as we all are.

John was on and off with God. He felt compelled to seek God, and in some periods of his life, he believed the gospel truth about Jesus Christ who died on the cross in order to make unholy people holy. John believed, but not enough to live for Christ.

"Be holy for I am holy." How could John do that after bobbing in and out of Christianity? What power could ever free him from his slavery to himself? The answer was the power of the gospel. Because the gospel is inspired by the Holy Spirit of God, John Chambers was transformed when he heard that gospel message enough times.

According to the Scriptures, this is the good news:

That at the right time Christ died for the ungodly. For one will hardly die for a righteous man; though perhaps for the good man someone would dare even to die. But God demonstrates His own love towards us, in that while we were yet sinners, Christ died for us. Much more then, having now been justified by His blood, we shall be saved from the wrath of God through Him. For if while we were enemies we were reconciled to God through the death of His Son, much more, having been reconciled, we shall be saved by His life (Romans 5:6-10).

Over and over again, John had been listening to the truth of what Jesus did. Then he got cancer. He said that his cancer is what healed him. After he was diagnosed, he finally became willing to let go of the worldliness that had snared him. He apologized to his kids, saying he was sorry for not paying attention as they grew up; he became generous with his money; he funded a Bible translation for a people group who beforehand had no access to God's Word in their own language; he took mission trips to Africa; he prayed more and prayed consistently; he listened with interest to what his grown children had to say; he treated his fourth wife kindly; and he teared up often due to his gratitude for the forgiveness God had shown him. He went from being unholy to being holy. I bore eyewitness of that—because John Chambers was my dad.

When I was little, my dad used to trivialize my problems. When I was older, before he died, Daddy (that's what I called him) was there to help me with the biggest challenge I ever faced. Though it took him sixty-eight years, it was not too late for him to trust in Jesus, and to live accordingly. It was not too late for him to regard God as his *reference point* and worship God as King, as his First Love.

You Can Become Holy

It's not too late for you either. And it's not too late for me. Today is the day that you can become holy by trading your sin-stained self for a purified holy self. You'll still be you, but you'll be new. You'll be different. You'll be better because you'll see God as your Holy Father who loves you with holy love.

Holy people know they are forgiven. Holy people know that being holy is impossible outside of a relationship with God. If you want to become holy, then you must put your faith in God. You must choose to trust, not blindly but with your heart and soul and mind—that it's true that God loves you personally. In other words, you yourself must be more truthful.

Holiness requires us to be truthful about ourselves, so that we can be amazed at God's love. To be holy is to accept the love of God.

My dad accepted God's love in his final years. That's how he found the strength to turn away from evil and do what is good. In the last years of his life, Daddy didn't wonder if he was a Christian anymore. He knew he was a Christian because he knew the love of God. For the first time in his life, he no longer made excuses for himself. He accepted God's grace and marveled at God's forbearance and generosity.

My dad trusted in God's forgiveness. That's what made him holy on his deathbed. God made him holy, and the holiness of his death—of the way he died—set him apart.

There's a word in the Spanish language called *sonrisa*. The word *sonrisa* means "smile." It's my favorite word in Spanish because *sonrisa* sounds in English like the word *sunrise*. Except *sonrisa* is spelled s-o-n-r-i-s-a, like the rising of the Son who was resurrected on the third day. Isn't that a great word for "smile"? When people smile, their whole face changes. A smile brightens a face as the sunshine in the morning lights the day.

When I think of my fathers' death, I can feel a holy smile rising from my core up to my face. I can't help but smile because of the inexplicable joy that I feel when I recall my father's death. My dad, John Chambers, entrusted himself to God so vividly that it's worth telling you in detail what that looked like.

A Death Observed

My father's death was rather sudden. One morning he was fine (as far as "fine" goes for someone with stage four cancer). He ate breakfast; he brushed his teeth; he combed his hair. But then, out of nowhere, a fierce pain stabbed him in his side. Turns out, it was a pain in Daddy's lung. Overnight he had come down with double pneumonia. Thanks to his wife Barbara's insistence, he agreed to be rushed to the hospital.

In a matter of forty-five minutes, my dad was on life support. He would've died that day had he not gone straight away to the emergency room.

Daddy never got to talk to us again—not in words. But he communicated. And his communication was the sweetest sign of faith I've ever seen.

Providentially I got to be with him; I made it from California to Texas before he passed. I was scheduled to fly to Capetown, South Africa, but when Daddy was suddenly ambushed by that piercing pain, I couldn't get myself to go on an international trip. For months, almost a year, I had looked forward to going to Africa to the 2010 Lausanne Congress on World Evangelization, a meeting that only happens every twenty years or so. And though everyone who advised me, including my dad's wife, told me to keep my plan to go to Africa, I didn't have a sense of peace about doing that.

My dad was in a coma, they said. "He won't even know you're there if you come visit him," someone added. "Just come to Texas when you get back," said someone else.

I was so overwhelmed that basically I froze and stayed at home a few more days, stalling with ambivalence about going to Texas or to Capetown. But then a *kairos* moment came when suddenly I felt prompted to catch a flight to Texas right away. That was one of the best decisions I've ever made.

It was Monday, October 18, 2010, when I finally arrived at the hospital. For five days my dad had been laid up in intensive care. He had been sleeping, that is, heaving while resting in sedation the whole time. Not once had he responded in any detectable way to anyone who had tried to talk to him.

It was hard for me to view him. I burst into tears as I tried even to recognize my dad. He was bloated and inflated, yet so punctured. He had four different intravenous needles inserted into his neck, a larger needle imposed into his groin, and tubes filled with food pushed into his nostrils. His body was so swollen that the proportion of his features were all distorted. Purple was the color of his arms. His arms were purple because they were bruised from the pressure of so much water rushing through his pores as a result of having two failed kidneys. He had tubes in every orifice, except for his eyes and ears. The worst one was in his mouth—it was a breathing ventilator, like a vacuum cleaner hose, shoved down into his throat. The hose was saving his life, though it was causing him to gasp with every heaving breath as wafts of air were pumped into his lungs.

In watching death overtake him, I could only begin to imagine how disturbing it must have been to watch Jesus surrender to death upon the cross. Granted, Jesus had no needles in his neck. But He had needles in His head due to His mock crown of thorns. Our Lord Jesus had nails, not needles, in his hands. A sword, not a needle, in His side.

I never realized until seeing my dying father that I never had been taught what *die* means. I knew what *death* means. Death is an evil, an enemy God employs to further illustrate God's grace. Death puts an end to the suffering of this life in all its fallenness. Death closes the door; it puts a limit on the pain that any one person might endure. Death is the opposite of life.

But what does it mean to die? I had never seen anyone die. As Christians we glibly say that Jesus died. Now my father was dying, and it made me think of Jesus more realistically.

I was filled with such emotion that I found myself repeatedly saying to my dad, "Daddy, I love you. Thank you for hanging on so I could be here with you. Thank you for showing me what it's like to die—for showing me what Jesus did."

In watching my dad die, I could only begin to imagine how disturbing it must have been to watch Jesus surrender to death upon the cross. Granted, Jesus had no needles in his neck. But He had needles in His head, a mock crown of thorns. Our Lord Jesus had nails, not needles, in his hands. A sword, not a needle, in His side.

I already knew from Jesus' example that it's possible for a person to die in faith. Now my dad was doing that. My repentant dad was demonstrating that Christ's victory over death assists us in our dying, if only we will believe—if only we will trust in God's amazing grace and assurance that we ourselves have been forgiven.

In the first half hour of my being there with my dad, I was caressing him, talking to him, assuring him of my love, when suddenly his eyes opened wide! Daddy looked at me! His pulse raced up from sedation level to 115 beats a minute. No one expected this, since he had hardly moved in the five days that he had been there. I've never felt more appreciated and loved. My dad heard my voice and opened his eyes! He kept staring at me in a way that no one has ever stared at me before.

I felt a terrible joy.

Somewhere in all my cascades of attempting to comfort him, my dad catapulted himself from the bed. He actually lifted his upper body from the bed in defiance of the ties that held his hands down like handcuffs, as if he had been arrested like Jesus. Sitting up in that hoisted position, my father's dilated eyes stared desperately into mine, penetrating the deepest part of me. I can't find the words to say how traumatized my father seemed to be. In that helpless look he gave me, with the humanity of a victim being tortured, he expressed *by far* the most pained countenance of any person I've ever seen. Nothing—nothing—nothing comes even close, that I have encountered, to being similar to the look upon Daddy's face. As far as I could tell, he was being gripped by the power of evil.

I called the nurse who increased his meds, so that he could calm down again. As soon as he settled down, I could no longer stand to stay in the room. Like everyone who fled when Jesus was hemmed in by the forces of darkness, I left the hospital room haunted by that look on Daddy's face. I didn't think I'd ever recover from having seen it. It was a look of utter, extreme, legitimate, pure suffering. That's what got me. I saw pain in a purified form. The most distilled pain I've ever seen. It stabbed me hard. It was violent, and it refused to be my dad's pain alone. I felt tainted by the presence of that evil. And the smell, the stench was awful. I almost gagged. I just had to get outside for some fresh air.

The Lord was near because, after praying in solitude, I felt bonded to my dad in a way that I never had before. Once I came back into his room, I didn't want to leave his side again.

At some point the doctor entered the room and said it would soon be over for my dad. In unequivocal language, the doctor said that shortly someone would need to tell the staff to remove the life support, since Daddy had requested for that to be done if he continued to be unable to live without the assistance of a machine. So Barbara, my dad's wife, said she didn't have the strength to be that someone. So the plan from that point on was for my brother and I to serve as Daddy's farewell team.

Daddy's Farewell Team

As I waited for my brother to arrive, I began to pray that we would see God. Later that night, we *did* see God. We saw the Lord through our eyes of faith. Though Daddy lived six years longer than the doctor said he would, cancer still stole his life. But it did not steal his faith.

Even though my dad was sedated in deep sleep, it was heartbreaking to leave him in order to pick up my brother from the airport. My brother was flying in from Singapore. About an hour or two before midnight, my brother's plane landed. All day long I had been trying to help our father hang on a little longer through the heaving, heavy minutes until my brother and I together could send him off.

"Just thirteen more hours, Daddy! And then you fly away to be with Jesus, okay? Just eight more hours . . . Just three more hours, Daddy. I'm so proud of you. And I'm here to confirm that you did not give up. You're fighting to the end. You're staying the course. You're doing great; you're doing great. You're waiting for your son. This is a big gift to your son. Thank you also for giving this gift to me, Daddy."

When my brother and I arrived at the hospital together around 1:00 a.m., we had the most memorable experience. In order to be brief, I'll just say this: My brother needed some time to get acclimated to Daddy's body and deathbed. His process of adjusting reminded me of my own.

In keeping with our plan, my brother and I soon transitioned into a full-on worship service. And Daddy was awake for it. For two hours straight, we tended to our dad, singing hymns, praying, quoting Scripture, assuring him, and mingling our tears physically with his. Can you believe that? Once we started worshiping, Daddy somehow shed tears.

Being at my dad's bedside wasn't quite the same with my brother there. I wish everyone in the world could know my brother. He's as funny as my dad, and just as bad of a singer. As we neared the very end of that precious worship time, my hilarious wonderful brother leaned into Daddy's half-deaf ear and said loudly in a jovial voice, "Dad, you're about to go to a place where you can carry a tune!"

And you know what John Chambers did?

He smiled! Even with that hose—that vacuum cleaner—rammed inside his mouth. He smiled in spite of everything. His smile looked like a halo around that hose.

I will never forget that smile, that miraculous *sonrisa*. Daddy's deathbed-*sonrisa* resounded the good news of the miracle of Jesus' resurrection. Jesus Christ has risen from the dead! He rose up like the sunrise and brightened every crevice of this darkened universe. Jesus conquered sin *and* death—my father's sin and death—and yours and mine. By grace, my dad believed that. He knew in his dire hour that Jesus Christ had saved him and that his immediate future was secure.

I had prayed that we'd see God. When I saw Daddy's smile, his beautiful *sonrisa*, that's when I believe I saw the Lord. That smile was set apart. It was heavenly. It was holy. And it slam-dunked the evil that had gripped my father earlier when he had looked at me so desperately before.

That smile was downright glorious. I'll never be the same on account of seeing it.

Once I saw that smile, I soon realized that Mel Gibson probably missed it when, in *The Passion of the Christ,* he showed Jesus on the cross—all gloom. I could be wrong, but I have a hunch that when Jesus hung on the cross, He smiled too. It's not explicitly stated in the Scriptures, but I think it makes sense: When the repentant thief, being crucified on the cross right next to Jesus, called out to Jesus, Jesus gazed at him and said with a victory smile, "today you shall be with Me in Paradise" (Luke 23:43).

If my dad could smile in his agony at my brother and me, then I believe that Jesus could smile in His agony too. Jesus loved that thief who humbly spoke the truth right before it was too late. Can you imagine how Jesus felt when He heard that thief's confession? According to Luke 15, heaven rejoices when one person comes to faith. When that thief repented, I think Jesus smiled. I even think that thief smiled too.

Holy moments. Holy smiles. Holy confessions of faith that form us into the image of Jesus Christ. God made my father holy because my dad looked to God. He trusted God when my brother cracked that joke.

The hospital workers soon joined us in order to remove that horrible hose and then pull that endless tube out from Daddy's nose. Everything happened so fast, yet it seemed so utterly vivid from second to second to second. Once all the medical equipment was detached from Daddy's body, his hard labor was to breathe. He seemed exhausted. A matter of minutes later, he ended with a sigh that sounded like a sigh of relief.

My father died with his face in my hand. On the other side of the bed, my brother was touching his shoulder and holding his other hand, and the two of us said good-bye as God whisked our dad away.

I'm so glad I went to Texas. I can't wait to go to heaven and debrief that holy episode with my dad. I'm so curious to find out what the experience was like from his perspective.

Death Is Swallowed Up in Victory

From my perspective, the whole thing was amazing. Thanks to our time with Daddy, I am more amazed that Jesus *died*. He laid down His life, and He took it up again (John 10:17). He conquered death by rising from the dead.

The prophet Isaiah and the apostle Paul both announced Jesus' triumph: "Death is swallowed up in victory" (Isaiah 25:8, I Corinthians 15:54).

"Thanks be to God," said the apostle Paul, "Who gives us the victory through our Lord Jesus Christ!" (I Corinthians 15:57).

Daddy's life ended in victory. By faith, my prodigal father became holy.

It is not too late for us to be holy. It's not too late for us to pray this prayer today:

> *Holy God, I pray for forgiveness, even though I know I don't deserve it. I want to be holy, not tainted. I've soiled my soul with sin, and I want to be cleansed by the precious blood of Jesus Who died for Sarah's dad and for me too. Set my heart aflame. Fill me with Your love. Please help me to believe You really love me. I'm sorry for my selfishness and hardness. Please give me the motivation to be truthful and non-defensive from now on. You are a great God. All glory be to God! Thank*

You for being so patient that You waited for me to find out that it's not too late for be holy as You are holy. In Jesus' Name I pray, Amen.

Part 5

Holy Practices

Sermon 13

Holiness Takes Practice

T. Scott Daniels

What then? Should we sin because we are not under law but under grace? By no means! Do you not know that if you present yourselves to anyone as obedient slaves, you are slaves of the one whom you obey, either of sin, which leads to death, or of obedience, which leads to righteousness? But thanks be to God that you, having once been slaves of sin, have become obedient from the heart to the form of teaching to which you were entrusted, and that you, having been set free from sin, have become slaves of righteousness. I am speaking in human terms because of your natural limitations. For just as you once presented your members as slaves to impurity and to greater and greater iniquity, so now present your members as slaves to righteousness for sanctification.

When you were slaves of sin, you were free in regard to righteousness. So what advantage did you then get from the things of which you now are ashamed? The end of those things is death. But now that you have been freed from sin and enslaved to God, the advantage you get is sanctification. The end is eternal life. For the wages of sin is death, but the free gift of God is eternal life in Christ Jesus our Lord (Romans 6:15-23, NRSV).

Right after Debbie and I married in 1990, I decided that I needed to take up running. There were several reasons why I decided to become a runner. My first concern was that I would gain what many of my already married friends called the "first year fifteen." Meaning most of them had gained fifteen pounds in their first year of marriage as they moved from the eat-when-you-can life of the single man to the home cooking of the newly married. But I also wanted to prove to my family (and to myself) that somewhere deep inside of me was an athlete just dying to get out.

So I went to a well-known running store and purchased the best pair of running shoes I could afford. I subscribed to *Runners World Magazine* and read each issue cover to cover. And in a great step of faith I signed up to run in a top flight half marathon scheduled on Labor Day—giving me a full six months to train.

The only problem was a combination of procrastination and a lack of time. I was serving as a youth minister in Seattle at the time and ended up having the kind of summer youth ministers usually have. Meaning, I went to camps, retreats, and mission trips all through the summer, but I didn't get in much training. By the time Labor Day rolled around, the longest run I had put in was eight miles. But I wasn't worried because I thought for sure that the adrenaline on race day could carry me the remaining 5.1 miles. An article in *Runners World* said to "carbo-load" the night before a big race, so Debbie made me a huge bowl of spaghetti. I felt ready to go.

The race began, and it was a wonderful feeling running with about ten thousand others. The first three miles I spent just trying not to get stepped on. I happened to see my new wife at the five-mile mark. Debbie looked very concerned. While she was waiting for me to pass, she had been talking to the spouses of some of the other runners. They were sharing some of the rigorous training that their spouses had gone through to get ready for the race. One of them asked Debbie what her husband had done? She said, "He ate a big bowl of spaghetti last night." She knew I was in trouble.

I got to the eight-mile mark and still felt okay. I was trying to find the marker for mile nine but couldn't see it. I asked the runner beside me where the course went next, and he pointed straight up the mountain. What I saw in front of me was a mile of switchbacks headed up a steep incline with the nine-mile marker at the very top. Now I knew I was in serious trouble.

The rest of the story is as long and painful as the next five miles were that day. Suffice it to say, I was passed by dozens of race walkers and people using walkers. The good news was that I finished the race. The bad news was that I finished right behind an 86-year-old woman who was also running her first half marathon.

Thrilled to be finished, I just stopped and collapsed. As soon as I straightened my legs, my muscles contracted, and I was no longer able to bend my knees. After several hours on the course I desperately needed to find a restroom. The day ended with my father carrying his grown son to the port-a-potty while saying, "Did you see that old lady who outran you?"

The point of the story is that one doesn't become a runner by purchasing the right shoes. And one doesn't become a runner by subscribing to the right magazine. A person becomes a runner by running... and running... and running some more. It is the practice of running that makes a person a runner.

Transformed by Grace

As a child of the Holiness Movement, I have been incredibly thankful for a theology that confesses that God in his grace does not just want to forgive us but transform us, by his grace, into the image of God we were created to be. But if there is a critique that I would make of the tradition in which I was raised and formed, it would be that holiness—or sanctification—was often thought of as primarily a crisis commitment that a person made that led to a one-time experience of being sanctified or made holy. This focus on holiness being received through a crisis experience with God's Spirit often left very little room or logic for the necessity of any form of spiritual discipline.

In his book *Responsible Grace*, historical theologian Randy Maddox makes the argument that the Anglicanism out of which John Wesley's Methodist movement began is an interesting hybrid blend of Protestant, Catholic, and Orthodox Christianity. As the Church of England (Anglicanism) was formed, argues Maddox, its founding theologians drew on the authority of Scripture and the primacy of faith from the Reformers. They retained many of the spiritual practices and forms of liturgy from Catholicism. And they returned to the early Eastern (Orthodox) Fathers theologically to draw on a theology of *theosis*—a doctrine that believes that Jesus Christ took on all that is human so that humanness in the body might be redeemed. In other words, Christ became like us so that we could be like him.

It is easy to recognize how the Protestant roots have remained a shaping force in the Methodist and subsequent Holiness traditions, and it is also easy to see how the roots of the Wesleyan and Holiness views of sanctification (or Christian perfection) are connected to the Orthodox *theosis* doctrine. But what was often lost in my own experience in the preaching and teaching of holiness was the more Catholic emphasis on the role of Christian practices and spiritual disciplines as a means of grace through which the Spirit of God matures and completes believers in the image of Christ.

Spiritual Disciplines

Any student of John Wesley will know that he continually emphasized not only the sacraments as significant means of grace through which the Spirit of God works to transform believers into the image of Christ, but he also regularly emphasized other spiritual disciplines—"methods"—through which God works to perfect or complete the love of God in the heart of the disciple. To state it plainly, for Wesley, holiness takes faith and trust, and it may often be experienced as a kind of crisis of commitment. But holiness also takes practice—or more properly, practices.

In Romans 6, Paul is in the midst of a complex theological argument about how and why the gospel has extended itself not only to Jews but to Gentiles as well. He is addressing the touchy issue of the end of the Law through the life, death, and resurrection of Jesus. The sixth chapter begins with addressing the question: If the Law has been put to death and grace has taken its place, can (or even should) a person keep on sinning so that grace can abound all the more?

To think that a person should keep on sinning so that grace can flow all the more is simply silly talk for Paul. What has really replaced the life lived under the Law is not lawlessness but the new creation of God's kingdom in and through Christ's resurrection.

Paul's theology in Romans hinges on the resurrection. There are places in the New Testament where the reader is informed of the dispute between the Pharisees and Sadducees over the issue of the resurrection of the dead. The Sadducees did not believe in the resurrection of the dead. (This is why they are "sad-you-see.") But it is most likely that they denied the resurrection because they feared that a belief in the resurrection of the dead would only energize and encourage zealots to act out violently against their oppressive leaders in the hope of reward after death, thus creating more political tension and oppression for the Jewish people. But for the Pharisees, like Paul, a commitment to the idea of the resurrection of the dead was essential.

For Paul, and likely for most of the Jewish faithful in the first century, the resurrection was the great event that would happen at the end of history when God would resurrect the dead and judgment would occur. So what is profound and world changing for Paul in the gospel is that the resurrection—that which should happen at the end of history—broke into history through the resurrection of Jesus. In the resurrection of Christ, the Eschaton—also known as the end of history—has now broken into the middle of history. Christ was resurrected from the dead as the first fruits not only of eternal life but as the beginning of the new creation: a creation where the Law has been put to death and where there is no longer Jew or Greek, slave or free, male or female, for we are all one in Christ Jesus (Galatians 3:28).

The New Creation

It is this reality of the new creation, here in Romans, that Paul is arguing the believer experiences in baptism. Paul writes, "Do you not know that all of us who have been baptized into Christ Jesus were baptized into his death? Therefore we have been buried with him by baptism into death, so that, just as Christ was raised from the dead by the glory of the Father, we too might walk in newness of life" (Romans 6:3-4). For Paul, like Israel, entered the waters of the Red Sea as slaves to the old order of Pharaoh; so too, the believer enters the water of baptism as slaves to sin and the Law. But in the same way that the Israelites exited the waters of the Red Sea freed from bondage to Pharaoh and became God's new nation and new people, so too the believer comes out of the waters of baptism sharing in the resurrection life of Christ, set free from sin, and now participating in the new creation.

In baptism the believer identifies with the death and resurrection of Jesus, and thus enters into the new creation. Both Jew and Gentile alike now share, through baptism and faith, in the eschatological life of the resurrection.

But there is a problem. The believer leaves the water as part of the new creation, but the world still seems in many ways like the same old place. There is still division between Jew and Greek. There is still tension between slave and free. There is still a lack of unity between male and female. And the believer quickly also discovers that some of the same patterns and habits of sin are still present even though she or he has made a commitment of faith and shared in the death and resurrection of Christ. Martin Luther often quipped that in baptism the old life is drowned, but we should remember that, "The Old Adam is a very good swimmer."

Because Adam is such a good swimmer, Paul implores the Roman believers to "present" the members of their body to God. Paul uses the word "present" six times between verses 13 and 19. And the verb tense of the word for "present" (*paristemi*), used in this passage in Greek, implies not just a one time presenting of the members of one's body to God but thinks of it as a continuous action—"so now present (and keep on presenting) your members as slaves to righteousness" (Romans 6:19).

I would paraphrase or summarize Paul's emphasis in the passage before us this way: *You used to be a slave to sin, and so each day you presented (and you kept on presenting) the members of your body to various practices that formed in you habits of brokenness and sin that often led to destruction and despair. But you have now been set free from that. You have died to your old way of life and have entered into the resurrection life of Jesus. So now, don't live like a slave to sin, but rather each day present (and keep on presenting) the members of your body to God as a servant of righteousness. And as you present your whole body to Christ in this way, you will participate in new practices and form new habits that will re-form in you the life of holiness to which you have been called.*

Holy Practices

So, how do we do that? How do we present our members daily to this new life? What are the practices that form in us the life of holiness?

The list of practices and spiritual disciplines that have been considered essential and helpful over the course of Christian history is too long to include in this message. But let me mention a few.

In the text from Romans, Paul is already celebrating the role baptism was playing in the life of believers in confirming bodily the work the Spirit was accomplishing in moving people from the old creation to the new. A few years ago I baptized a new believer with whom I have developed a close friendship. The first day I met Ryan, he wanted me to know that he was an agnostic. But he attended church occasionally because his wife was a Christian and because he found my sermons "rhetorically pleasing."

After a couple of years of friendship and conversation, Ryan committed his life to Christ and decided to be baptized on Easter Sunday. A few months later, he invited our family over for dinner, and I noticed in his front room that he had framed his baptism certificate with a picture of his baptism. He had even set it up on a shelf with candles around it as a kind of memorial. I remarked that he was the first person I had baptized who had built a shrine to the event. He responded that he had set it up that way so that every morning he could look at it and be reminded of his new life. "My new life in Christ is such a change from my old way of living," he remarked, "that I need a daily reminder that my old life has been put to death."

Without question, for John and Charles Wesley the primary practice in which we find the transforming work of God at play is in the sacrament of the Eucharist. In his great hymn "O the Depth of Love Divine," Charles Wesley wrote:

> *If chiefly here thou may'st be found,*
> *If now, e'en now we find Thee here;*
> *O let their joys like ours abound!*
> *Invite them to the royal cheer;*
> *Feed with imperishable food,*
> *And fill their raptur'd souls with God.*

In the practice of the Lord's Table, the people of God are becoming what they eat. The mystery of the Eucharist for Wesleyan Christians is not the transformation of the common elements of the bread and cup, but rather it is the transformation the Spirit, at work in the elements, enacts in the common people who partake of the meal.

I was recently speaking at a Christian college campus where an amazing two-year revival of sorts was going on amongst the students. A gifted student leader had turned the Wednesday night optional worship opportunity for students into not only a time of worship and reflection on the Scripture, but had put into practice ending every student service with the Eucharistic meal. Two years later, as I talked to faculty and administration, they all commented on the amazing spiritual growth that was taking place in the lives of the students who were attending these services. Even though they received no credit for coming, nearly every Wednesday night was overflowing with students connecting to Christ, connecting to each other, and responding to God's call for missional living.

I asked the administrative director for the spiritual life on campus if he had figured out the secret to this revival that was taking place among the student body. He replied, "My only answer is the Lord's Table. I suppose if we believe that the Eucharist is a means of God's grace, then we shouldn't be surprised that those who are partaking of the Body of Christ on a regular basis start living like his body day-to-day."

In the last couple of decades the movement towards small groups has become significant in many evangelical churches. I believe that this is in part a realization of our need for accountability, community, and support. Wesley and the early Methodists intentionally connected Christians into classes and bands where they could not only share life together but where they could confess their sins to one another. Protestant reaction to Catholicism has unfortunately marginalized at times the important place for the confession of sin in the life of the believer. There have even been times in the Holiness tradition where confession was seen as unnecessary for the sanctified. But holiness—and our growth in grace—is largely dependent upon our need to remain accountable to others in the Body of Christ.

In his great work *Life Together*, Dietrich Bonhoeffer writes these great words about confession:

> In confession a [person] breaks through to certainty. Why is that it is often easier for us to confess our sins to God than to a brother [or sister]? God is holy and sinless, He is a just judge of evil and the enemy of all disobedience. But a brother [or sister] is sinful as we are. [They] know from their own experience the dark night of secret sin. Why should we not find it easier to go to a brother [or sister] than to the holy God? But if we do, we must ask ourselves whether we have not often been deceiving ourselves with our confession of sin to God, whether we have not rather been confessing our sins to ourselves and also granting ourselves absolution. And is not the reason perhaps for our countless relapses and the feebleness of our Christian obedience to be found precisely in the fact that we are living on self-forgiveness and not a real forgiveness? Self-forgiveness can never lead to a breach with sin; this can be accomplished only by the judging and pardoning Word of God itself.

The line I love is the last: "Self-forgiveness can never lead to a breach with sin." For Bonhoeffer, the communal practice of confession and forgiveness becomes one means among many others through which the breach from the old life and the transition into the new life is accomplished.

There are many other practices and disciplines that I could list. We could include worship, fasting, silence, prayer, Scripture reading, and many, many more. I hope that even this sermon, as an act of speaking for God and listening to his Spirit, is also a practice through which his purposes are being accomplished in us.

Conclusion

Paul ends Romans 6 by saying the benefit that we get from continually presenting the members of our body to Christ for righteousness is sanctification. This is the goal—to be sanctified or set apart for the unique and holy purposes of God in the world. To borrow another metaphor from the writer of Hebrews, the sanctified purpose to which we are called is to run the race Christ has set before us. But you don't become a runner by buying the right shoes and subscribing to the right magazine. You become a runner because you run.

In the same way, holiness requires faith in the sanctifying work of God and response to his grace. But you don't become holy by just making the right commitments. Holiness takes practice(s).

Sermon 14

Sanctify Them in the Truth; Your Word Is Truth

Timothy Finlay

Sanctify them in the truth; your word is truth (John 17:17, NRSV).

This Scripture, which links holiness or sanctification with truth and with the word of God, appears in Jesus Christ's moving prayer to the Father in John 17. The setting is the night before Jesus's crucifixion. After the last supper (John 13), Jesus gives what has become known as "the farewell discourse" (John 14-17) in which he expounds upon the reason for his imminent departure and upon the work of the Holy Spirit. Then, in John 17, we read the longest prayer of Jesus recorded in the Gospels in which he expresses his concern for the disciples after he has departed: "And now I am no longer in the world, but they are in the world, and I am coming to you. Holy Father, protect them in your name that you have given me, so that they may be one, as we are one" (John 17:11, NRSV). Even though the disciples are *in* the world (verse 11), they do not "belong to the world" (verses 14, 16).

It is at this point that Jesus requests of the Father: "Sanctify them in the truth" (verse 17). This verse inspired Charles Wesley, a founder of the Methodist movement, to write the following magnificent hymn:

That Spirit pure of truth and love,
That sacred unction from above

> *Did Thy first messengers ordain;*
> *It set them for Thyself apart,*
> *Reveal'd Thy word to every heart,*
> *And cleansed their lives from every stain:*
> *Still by the gospel word applied,*
> *Thy ministers are sanctified,*
> *The truth they lovingly receive,*
> *It saves their souls and sets them free;*
> *And consecrated, Lord, to Thee,*
> *Thy holy word they preach and live.*

The disciples are sanctified, set apart, made holy by the truth they lovingly receive.

How does this happen? The Gospel of John tells us a good deal about truth. So what is the link between truth and sanctification? We begin with what we can learn from the Old Testament about truth, because Jesus's teachings do not contradict the Hebrew Scriptures, even as they add new elements.

Truth and the Scriptures

The Queen of Sheba heard a report about Solomon's accomplishments and wisdom, and decided to find out whether it was true. She found this out, not by deciding whether it was pragmatic or useful to believe as true, nor by examining whether it was coherent with her other beliefs, but by travelling to Jerusalem and finding out whether the report corresponded to reality, to the way things actually were. The Queen of Sheba observed first-hand all the wisdom of Solomon and what he had achieved (1 Kings 10:4-5). She heard all the answers to her hardest questions (verse 3). And she said to Solomon, "The report was true that I heard in my own land of your accomplishments and of your wisdom, but I did not believe the reports until I came and my own eyes had seen it" (verse 6).

We see this same concept several times in Deuteronomy. If you hear a report that people are leading a city to serve other gods, "then you shall inquire and make search and ask diligently. And behold, if it be true and certain that such an abomination has been done among you, you shall surely put the inhabitants of that city to the sword"

(Deuteronomy 13:14-15). Again, concerning a report about a man or woman who worships other gods, "[If] you hear of it, then you shall inquire diligently, and if it is true and certain that such an abomination has been done in Israel, then you shall bring out to your gates that man or woman who has done this evil thing, and you shall stone that man or woman to death with stones" (Deuteronomy 17:4-5). The same procedure occurs in Deuteronomy 19:16-19 and 22:20-21. So a report, claim, or assertion is shown to be true if it corresponds to what is the case or what has been done, to reality in other words. If an assertion does not correspond with reality, then it is false.

Just as in ancient Israel, people in all societies instinctively know the meanings of "true reports" or "false reports." But it was in ancient Greece that the first philosophical discussion of the nature of truth arose. And in ancient Greece, there were three basic schools of thought concerning truth and the nature of reality. First, the materialists, such as Democritus and later the school of the Epicureans, believed that everything which existed was made of matter, that nothing non-material existed and that therefore there were no "facts" concerning anything non-material. Second, the Sophists went further and denied the very existence of truth—one of them said that there was no reality, that even if there were we could not know it, and that even if we could know it, we could not communicate that knowledge. So the Sophists said that all that mattered was the pragmatic, persuading other people to do what you want via rhetoric (the word "sophistry" comes from this approach), because truth did not exist.

It is obvious that these two schools of thought are in serious opposition to the Bible. To use Charles Wesley's words, "that Spirit pure of Truth and Love" that set apart or sanctified the disciples is not a material entity. Nor is "the gospel word" an entirely material thing but something of "spirit and life" (John 6:63). And the purpose of the Bible is to communicate to us knowledge about the ultimate reality. John's frequent use of the words "know" and "knowledge" is an emphatic rejection of the doctrine of the Sophists and their recent followers such as Nietzsche and Foucault.

But there was a third school of thought in ancient Greece—that of Socrates, Plato, Aristotle, and their followers—which vigorously argued that truth did exist, that a true assertion was one that corresponded to reality, and that a false assertion was one that did not. For example, in *Metaphysics*, Aristotle said, "To say of what is that it is not, or of what is not that it is, is false, while to say of what is that it is, and of what is not that it is not, is true," and there are similar statements by Plato in works such as *Cratylus* and *Sophist*. In *Categories*, Aristotle gives a more fully developed account of what has come to be known as "the correspondence theory of truth." The medieval theologian Thomas Aquinas restated it: "A judgment is said to be true when it conforms to the external reality" ("Of Truth," *Summa Theologica*). There is no evidence that the early or medieval Church was ever in opposition to this common sense approach to truth.

Perhaps even more importantly, Socrates, Aristotle and Plato believed that many of the most important truths concerned the non-material, in sharp distinction to the materialists. Facts concerning the immortality of the soul or the cardinal virtues of prudence, justice, courage, and temperance were greater truths than the mere empirical facts that were the only truths accepted by the materialists—from Democritus and the Epicureans to Richard Dawkins and Alex Rosenberg. Historically, the Christian church—though rejecting many of the specifics of the philosophical systems of Socrates, Plato and Aristotle—has agreed with the concept that there is truth, that truth is that which corresponds to reality, and that many of the most important truths concern the non-material.

Truth and Sanctification

Some truths have more to do with sanctification than other truths. The main connection between sanctification and truth lies in the second half of John 17:17, the part that tells us "Your word is truth." All truth is ultimately God's truth, but there is a difference between truth that is part of natural revelation and truth that is part of special revelation, especially Scripture.

God is concerned with all nations and made it possible for them to know the most basic moral laws without special revelation. We see some of the laws in the Old Testament in Hammurabi's law-code and other law-codes that preceded God's giving of the Torah on Mt. Sinai. And keeping these basic laws that are knowable through natural revelation leads to a certain level of holy living.

But God purposed to elect a peculiar people, beginning with Abraham and Sarah, continuing with Isaac and Rebekah, and then Jacob and Leah and Rachel from whom the children of Israel were descended. God set this people apart in a special covenant relationship. The people of Israel were to be peculiarly holy to God, and God revealed to them special truths—commandments, precepts, and statutes concerning how to live and concerning the ways of the Lord—that were recorded in Israel's Scriptures. These truths are known as special revelation, and it is this special revelation that is being primarily referenced here as "Your word is truth."

Perhaps the greatest psalm discussing God's word is Psalm 119. This is a magnificent acrostic poem consisting of twenty-two stanzas of eight verses each (eight verses beginning with the first Hebrew letter *aleph*, then eight verses beginning with the next Hebrew letter *beth*, and so on for all twenty-two letters of the Hebrew alphabet). And almost every one of its 176 verses contains at least one of the following Hebrew words: *torah* (law or instruction), *mitzvah* (commandment), *derek* (way), *eduth* (testimony or decree), *piqqud* (precept), *dabar* (word), *mishpat* (judgment or ordinance), *imrah* (saying) or *choq* (statute). The psalm begins as a meditation: "Happy are those whose way is blameless, who walk in the law of the Lord. Happy are those who keep his decrees, who seek him with their whole heart, who also do no wrong, but walk in his ways" (Psalm 119:1-3). But it soon turns into a personal prayer to God, in which the psalmist focuses on "your precepts" (verse 4), "your statutes" (verse 5), "your commandments" (verse 6), "your ordinances" (verse 7), and "your statutes" (verse 8).

I have a Bible in which these key words of Psalm 119 are highlighted in different colors. It aids my prayerful reading of the psalm, and I imagine a fugue of related motifs concerning God's word rising to God in prayer. But because we are concentrating on the phrase "your word" in this sermon, let us see what Psalm 119 says about *dabar* (word). The very first reference to *dabar* in Psalm 119 has a connection with holiness: "How can young people keep their way pure? By guarding it according to your word" (verse 9). Elsewhere, the psalmist pledges: "I will not forget your word" (verse 16), pleads: "revive me according to your word" (verse 25), implores: "strengthen me according to your word" (verse 28), demonstrates faith: "I trust in your word" (verse

42), reminds God: "remember your word to your servant" (verse 49), emphasizes hope: "I hope in your word" (verses 81, 114; see also verses 74, 147), praises the immutability of God and God's word: "The Lord exists forever; your word is firmly fixed in heaven" (verse 89), and asks for understanding: "according to your word" (verse 169). And we see an anticipation of John 17:17, when the psalmist writes: "The sum of your word is truth; and every one of your righteous ordinances endures forever" (Psalm 119:160).

Meditating upon God's word in the Scriptures is a vitally important spiritual discipline. Pondering the greatness of God's way of life helps us to live a more holy life ourselves. Further, we are to hope in God's word and trust in God's word; God's word contains promises in which we can have absolute trust. These promises ultimately concern the hope of eternal life through Jesus Christ, the son whom God sent into the world. Jesus tells the Father that the disciples "have believed that you sent me" (John 17:8). Believing is supremely important; right practice is not enough: "Those who believe in [the Son] are not condemned; but those who do not believe are condemned already, because they have not believed in the name of the only Son of God" (John 3:18).

Believing is directed here not to a thought or judgment (as in John 17:8), but to a person, Jesus. And this Jesus proclaimed, "I am the truth and the way and the life" (John 14:6). And the church, while retaining the correspondence understanding of truth as it pertained to thoughts, assertions or judgments, expanded the concept of truth to apply to humans, animals, or even inanimate things. A thing or object was true if it was a reliable (a concept of truth that one finds partly reflected in the Old Testament's usage of *'emet*). Thomas Aquinas defined truth as the equation of thing and intellect. In Question 16 ("Of Truth") in the first part of *Summa Theologica*, Aquinas argues: "The definition that Truth is the equation of thought and thing is applicable to it under either aspect." Both these aspects—judgment/assertion truths and person/thing truths—were regarded as ultimately deriving from God.

Conclusion

It is in Jesus that sanctification and truth meet. One of today's most popular hymns, which derives from a verse in Psalm 119, is "Thy word is a lamp unto my feet, And a light unto my path." Meditating upon God's word means meditating upon the Logos—the Word—the one in Whom "was life, and the life was the light of all people. The light shines in the darkness, and the darkness did not overcome it" (John 1:4-5). And the Word, Jesus, repeated the connection between sanctification and truth as follows: "And for their sakes I sanctify myself, so that they also may be sanctified in truth" (John 17:19). Jesus committed himself to God's holy will (sanctified himself) even to death on a cross so that the disciples would also be sanctified in the truth. To be sanctified followers of Jesus, to be willing to take up our cross, we have to be totally committed; we have to *believe* that "the gospel word" corresponds to reality, that Jesus is the way and the truth and the life.

Sermon 15

Spiritual Formation in an Age of YOLO: 'You Only Live Once'

Keith J. Matthews

2 Corinthians 4:16-18

It's a gift to speak with you on a topic that has been a passion of my heart, for much of my adult life. While I've been teaching and training pastors for the past nine years in the Graduate School of Theology, my sense of urgency and concern over the topic of *spiritual formation* comes from over three and a half decades of ministry as a person in church leadership and as a pastor.

In this brief time, permit me to challenge you: What is it that you really believe about spiritual formation? NOT what you "profess to believe," but *really* believe? Lastly, I want to give you some insights on how you can cooperate with God's grace, and get involved with your own spiritual transformation. You see, I believe the world is longing to see real people embodying goodness, beauty and truth, not just talking about it!

So, back to our beliefs for just a second: When you believe something you "act as if it is true." We all live up to our beliefs. Just follow me around for a week and you'll get a glimpse of what I really believe; my behavior will bear witness to reality. *BUT*, we in the Christian church have for the past generation been primarily focused on making converts based on "professions" of belief in order to secure individuals' heavenly destination. While this gospel's concern is primaily on the afterlife, vast numbers of Christians wonder what to do with their present life. This is where the topic of spiritual formation comes into play: What about my present life?

Spiritual Formation

Spiritual formation is about becoming the kind of person whose beliefs and professions reflect the character and person of Jesus Christ, naturally, here and now, not just when you die.

As a parent of three adult children, there is nothing that makes a parent feel more proud and grateful as when their child make choices that are wise, kind and good, not because they must do it for me the parent. They have become the kind of person who naturally does it out of their own desire and choices. This is how God delights over us, watching the kind of person we become and celebrating our choices with us. The fruit of our life in God is the person we become.

Yet, we live in a world that radically works against this kind of formation. Bear with me as I simplify two world-views that every Christian must grapple with.

Two Belief Systems or Worldviews

1. *"YOLO"- "You only live once!"* Many people use this phrase on Twitter or Facebook, to imply that we should live each day as if it may be our last. If we die, since we don't come back to life again, then we should live our lives to our fullest now.

This belief system or world view at its worst, says, I alone am the master of my fate. Since life is only in my hands, I'll do what I want . . . "go for the gusto" right now, since there is only one life to live. In this framework there is no God, no consequences, just my needs to be fulfilled by my desires, right now! After all, "ya only live once!"

Now you may not fully embrace this mindset, but its philosophy has deep implications in the world today, and has made its way even into the minds of many Christians. Here's an example of what I mean.

Imagine with me that the medical community has now achieved the ability to do a brain transplant. Furthermore, imagine two medical gurneys each with Brittany Spears and Brad Pitt lying on each one.

Let's say they have just gone through a brain transplant; each of their bodies now with each other's brain. The surgery was successful, and they are now coming out of their anesthesia. Brad awakens first, but who wakes up? Brad or Brittany?

It never fails that, when I set this imaginary model up, people are generally confused and are baffled by the thought of what would be the result. Often the room is split down the middle with the real majority not knowing how to answer. It IS confusing, especially if you have adopted a physicalist or material view of the world

The belief for the Christian is that Brad would wake up! Why? Because Brad is not his brain! And, you are not your brain. What really makes you, You, is that you have a spirit, and it is eternal. Sorry to say that, when you die, your brain does not go with you. Do you really believe your thoughts of kindness and service and love originate with a chemical or electrical impulse? No, they come from your spirit, the executive center of the self, the originating factor in what makes you a person. So it is that, even within our Christian communities, we are deeply influenced by our culture, which is committed entirely to a physical or material view of the world.

One of PBS's biggest shows is Dr. Daniel Amen's "Change your Brain, Change your Life." I say: Change your life, and you will change you brain. But how do we do this? It begins with a vision, another world view . . .

2. *"You are a never-ending, never-ceasing spiritual being, with an eternal destiny, in God's Kingdom."* If you really believe this to be true, and not just profess it, then you will live a different way in this culture. Here's what the Apostle Paul believed:

> Therefore we do not lose heart. Though outwardly we are wasting away, yet inwardly we are being renewed day by day. For our light and momentary troubles are achieving for us an eternal glory that far outweighs them all. So we fix our eyes not on what is seen, but on what is unseen, since what is seen is temporary, but what is unseen is eternal (2 Corinthians 4:16-18, NIV).

Paul lived in this world-view. It is a world-view that sees people as eternal, never ceasing spiritual beings, who live life based on and nurtured in the unseen world called the Kingdom of God. This is a stark contrast from the YOLO worldview that is void of an eternal perspective with no divine purpose. It has no concern with the type of person we are becoming.

Our crying need today is people who have a sense of themselves through eternal lenses, a view of becoming a particular kind of person, for the good of the world. Sadly, even the best educational institutions are missing the mark.

A few year ago I heard the story of a young woman we will call Maria. Maria grew up in a small town with humble means, but she was so smart she received acceptance into Harvard. Even with scholarship money she had to work odd jobs cleaning dorm rooms to make ends meet. She enrolled in a large class with the famous Dr. Robert Coles, a well-known researcher and commentator on social and moral matters. She loved the class but melted into the woodwork of such a large course. During a class session she noticed the Teaching Assistant for the course, a student whose room she was assigned to clean. With regularity he proceeded to badger her sexually when she was working. She was humiliated and confounded by this student studying moral issues. So she went to Professor Coles and asked him this profound and important question: *"Dr. Coles, I've been taking all these philosophy courses, and we talk about what's true, what's important, and what's good. Well, how do you teach people to be good? What's the point of knowing good, but not becoming a good person?"*

Sadly, his response offered her no hope, and as the next semester began, she left the school confused and disillusioned. Her question resonates deeply in these current times. As Christians we might ask her question this way: *What's the point of knowing/believing/professing Christian truths, or even confessing your faith in Jesus, yet* not *becoming like Jesus?*

We have countless people sitting in our churches who have confessed Jesus Christ as Savior, who have received forgiveness of their sins, and secured their afterlife. Yet they have deep struggles in their present life in knowing how to become like Jesus in character and action. I believe spiritual formation is critical for change in our present life, but what are WE to do??

As a Pastor I Often Ask My Church These Two Questions

1. *How many of you really believe that your spiritual growth/transformation is of primary importance in your life?* Time after time when I ask this question to groups, the vast majority of people raise their hands affirming that it is a priority for their lives. But, then I ask this question...

2. *How many of you have a daily plan to fulfill this intention?* Very few raise their hands to this question. Overwhelming data shows that most Christians don't have a plan for their own transformation, often relying on the "osmosis" method of change. "The more I'm at church or chapel, the more I'll change one might say." But here's the truth about spiritual formation: *Everybody gets a spiritual formation! Hitler had a "formation," and so did Mother Theresa... and you're getting one too! Right now!*

The question we must ask is: How are we participating in our own formation with God? There is a part of your growth and transformation in Christ that is in YOUR hands. God is waiting on you! You must have a plan!

The Apostle Paul in 1 Tim. 4 writes his son in the faith, a young pastor named Timothy, and in sixteen short but potent verses Paul shares advice and a few commands to help him make it as a pastor: *"Have nothing to do with godless myths and old wives tales, rather... TRAIN YOURSELF TO BE GODLY. For physical training is of some value, but godliness has value for all things, holding promise for both the present life and the life to come"* (1 Timothy 4: 7, 8). We could say this another way to Timothy: "You must go to the spiritual gym and work out. If you don't, then no one will do it for you! But if you do, then it will save your ministry and carry you to eternity."

Another Truth to Bear in Mind: God is NOT opposed to EFFORT, but to EARNING!

Effort is an action; earning is an attitude! Your practice of spiritual disciplines/training is not works unless that's what you intend. Our participation in our transformation is critical, just as your plan for physical fitness for the reshaping of your body is critical. Listen to Paul's athletic imagery:

> Do you not know that in a race all the runners run, but only one gets the prize? Run in such a way as to get the prize. Everyone who competes in the games goes into strict training. They do it to get a crown that will not last, but we do it to get a crown that will last forever. Therefore I do not run like someone running aimlessly; I do not fight like a boxer beating the air. No, I strike a blow to my body and make it my slave so that after I have preached to others, I myself will not be disqualified for the prize (1 Corinthians 9: 24-27).

Even though we know these verses to be true, we often don't realize this core truth: *We tend to OVERESTIMATE what we can accomplish through TRYING, and UNDERESTIMATE what we can accomplish through TRAINING!*

Consider the following words, by John Joseph Surin: *"The chief reason people don't grow in their spiritual life is they give too big a place to indifferent things."* Yes, we must train ourselves spiritually, but we must train wisely with strategic intent. We have a wealth of writing historically on spiritual disciplines that aid us in our training. May it be that we together embrace this wonderful Christian world view, for our own change and others around us. The Lord knows we need it!

It is my hope that this "spiritual formation" might turn into a passionate, vibrant "spiritual formation life," filled with your own personal strategies in living life with God, which only you can do.

I pray that you will not only be filled with the knowledge of goodness, beauty, and truth, but that you will become a person of goodness, beauty, and truth as well.

So, remember these words throughout your day: *"I am a never-ending, never-ceasing spiritual being, with an eternal destiny, in God's Kingdom."*

Go in the peace and power of Christ!

Sermon 16

Prayer: God's Power-Sharing Device
[Preached on Father's Day]

Gary Black, Jr.

> If my people, who are called by my name, humble themselves, and pray, and seek my face, and turn from their wicked ways, then I will hear them from heaven, and forgive their sins and heal their land. (2 Chronicles 7:14, ESV)

If you are living in the world I'm living in and watching, reading about, and trying to grapple with the issues that we face in this generation, perhaps you, like me, may wonder, when thinking back to the founding of the United States—after all things are considered—it may be more difficult, more challenging, more taxing to be a follower of Jesus today than in any previous American generation. Now, please don't hear me say that I believe being a follower of Jesus Christ here in the United States is more difficult and dangerous than it is to be a disciple and profess Christ in Iran, Darfur, or North Korea. The church in America is overwhelmingly blessed, prosperous, and virtually free of overt, physical persecution. But what I do wonder about is whether the values and beliefs that many American's have counted on or relied on in the past, which have been woven, over time and with much sacrifice, into the fabric of our daily lives by those who came before us, now seem to be fraying at the edges and losing their strength. If this is true, then I suggest this is in part what the Chronicler in 2 Chronicles 7:14 is suggesting or hinting had occurred in his time, as well.

When I started to think and pray for what I hope will be a word of encouragement to you on Father's day, I took a long hard look at my own life as a Christian man, a husband, a father of two daughters, as well as my experience of now forty-plus years in and around others within the church, I asked myself the question almost all leaders ask: Where can I, where can we improve?

I started by asking a key question of several of my friends and associates, some professors, some students, some pastors, and many of their spouses. I asked each the same question: Give me three areas where you think Christian men can and should improve. Without exception, the one common denominator they all listed was prayer. I remember the wife of a friend of mine listed only one without hesitation: "Prayer. That's it. No second or third choice. PRAYER!" I think she's right. Now, I know that a few dozen people are not a CNN/Gallup poll, nor anything remotely scientific. But I'm suggesting the clincher for me was the bell that went off in my heart when she said "prayer" because I know it's absolutely true in my life. Someone once told me that, if you preach to your weaknesses, then you will never run out of material! So that's what I plan to do: to speak from my own experience and struggles with prayer, and try to convey the lessons I am trying to learn about through developing a life of prayer.

Developing a Life of Prayer

I certainly don't know all the reasons why we seem to struggle with prayer. There may be as many reasons as there are people. And certainly not all of us struggle with prayer equally or at the same level. But in some ways, prayer seems to be something of a universal issue for many of us. I suspect that my difficulty with prayer stems at least from some direct connection with my inability or my absolute disdain for stopping and asking for directions when I get lost. Perhaps that is the same gene in me that keeps me from reading the instructions before I try to assemble a toy or bicycle on Christmas Eve.

Awhile back, my wife and I bought a car, and the salesman wanted to go through every page of the owner's manual with me before we left the dealership. I was about to lose my mind as he went page by page through a fairly thick owner's manual. I've been driving cars since, well, honestly, since a little before I got my license, and I've owned and driven a fair number of different automobiles. So I had no desire to start at such a late age having an owner's manual read to me. But a couple weeks ago, we were cleaning out our car, and my wife Susie wanted to turn off the inside dome light so we didn't run down the battery. I didn't know how to turn off the interior lights. So I'm looking at all the buttons and switches and trying to open and close doors and switch the ignition on and off, and what is she doing? She's over there reading the owner's manual.

I think that many men, if we are honest, can identify with that simple story because we too often become overly confident in our own abilities to accomplish our responsibilities. For me, I think most of this confidence comes from the belief that, if you give me enough time and opportunity to get something right, then I'm pretty optimistic I'll get it right or fix it eventually. Kind of like the idea that even a blind squirrel will find an acorn eventually. But, again, if I'm transparent, then I have to admit I tend to be a little overly optimistic when it comes to evaluating my own skills. Are you? We also have a tendency at times, all of us, to be a little stubborn and proud. So, those attributes can naturally morph over into our spiritual lives and our thinking about prayer.

Let me be serious for a moment and say this, and I know it might be bold and uncomfortable. But I believe the continued practice of ignoring the essential nature of prayer can be, and in my case I think it was, one of the ultimate signs of a life consumed by arrogance and pride. You see, I don't ask for advice, assistance, direction, or help if I truly don't think I need it. One has to be either humble or accurately in touch with the circumstances around them, or both, to ask for help. But to ignore or not even consider seeking the direction and counsel of the great and loving God of the universe who has made himself available to me in a new and living way is to make the gravest of errors in the presumption of my abilities, the accuracy of my perspectives, and the depth of my wisdom, which, I must admit, has often left me worse off than I was before. And thus very often my own best efforts and talents carry little or no value at all in terms of solving my problems or achieving the kind of thriving in life I desire. One of the hardest lessons of human existence is learning that in the end, the most crucial problems we face in human existence do not have a human solution.

Understanding Prayer

So what was my flaw? My flaw was then and too often is still the same today: I didn't really understand prayer. And may I say that in talking with several men around me, that I respect, and who sincerely love God and are devoted to his causes, they also admitted to not really understanding prayer either. Now you might say, "Come on. Everybody knows that prayer is simply talking to God. How can something so easy not be understood?" Well let's just consider that for a few minutes. There is hope for us because we have a brilliant master teacher and instructor who gave us a perfect answer to this troubling question. And we can see in the gospels that Jesus' disciples really didn't understand prayer either.

So let's turn again to 2 Chronicles 7:14. This is a fairly famous verse, but let me give you just a brief refresher on the books of Chronicles. We think these books were written shortly after the Babylonians conquered Jerusalem, then destroyed the temple, and kicked the Jews out of their own land. And the writer, possibly Ezra, is recalling the good old days of the heights of the kingdom when David and Solomon reigned as kings. Chronicles reminds me a little bit of Tom Brokaw's famous book that came out several years ago about the *Greatest Generation*. He reflects on the leaders and the accomplishments that were achieved by those born roughly at the turn of the century, around 1900: The "Good Old Days" as they have been called. These are the good old days for the Kingdom of Israel recorded for us in 1 & 2 Chronicles. They were not perfect days, but for most Jews they were very good days. Consider 2 Chronicles 7:8-14:

> At that time Solomon held the feast for seven days, and all Israel with him, a very great assembly, from Lebo-hamath to the Brook of Egypt. And on the eighth day they held a solemn assembly, for they had kept the dedication of the altar seven days and the feast seven days. On the twenty-third day of the seventh month he sent the people away to their homes, joyful and glad

of heart for the prosperity that the LORD had granted to David and to Solomon and to Israel his people.

Thus Solomon finished the house of the LORD and the king's house. All that Solomon had planned to do in the house of the LORD and in his own house he successfully accomplished. Then the LORD appeared to Solomon in the night and said to him: "I have heard your prayer and have chosen this place for myself as a house of sacrifice. When I shut up the heavens so that there is no rain, or command the locust to devour the land, or send pestilence among my people, if my people who are called by my name humble themselves, and pray and seek my face and turn from their wicked ways, then I will hear from heaven and will forgive their sin and heal their land."

The passage here is specifically recalling the very day the temple was dedicated to Yahweh, its grand opening, so to speak—after all the pomp and circumstance, after all the speeches made by men in funny hats, after all the feasts and food and wine are consumed and the people are home, tired from all the activities of the day and snug in their beds with smiles on their faces... you know the feeling. It's the feeling you have after you're home from a day at Disneyland, and the kids finally come down from their sugar high from the cotton candy, and you lay your head on your pillow with a smile on your face knowing you've done your job as a parent and created a memory. But, imagine now that you've been to Disneyland seven days in a row. You are really happy it's over.

Yet, this event is really much bigger than that, isn't it? It's bigger than we can really imagine. We don't have anything that would compare, and let us reflect on this amazing achievement for the people of Israel. This was a group of ex-slaves who wandered somewhat aimlessly around the desert for decades, who were despised by their neighbors, who were poor, weak, nomadic, and often thought of as having little or no consequence in their world. But now, this is the same people who, in a very short time, became the shining example of a prosperous, blessed, and sophisticated society. And this, the temple, was the crowning achievement in recognition of the God who chose them, called them, and caused his blessings to fall on them. This was a big week of events. And so you can imagine a little bit how Solomon might have been feeling that night—a little bit of amazement and gratefulness and probably a feeling of being totally unworthy to be the man who was king when the temple was completed. I don't think Solomon was the kind of guy who was born on third base but thought he earned a triple. I think Solomon was barely able to contain his sense of the spiritual weight, the *kabod*, the glory of God, as it was displayed in and around him and his people.

So.... what is God saying here? We must remember: This is a mostly agrarian society of farmers and herders. If the rain is shut off, then you lose your crops, and you lose your grazing grasses. Then if the locusts come, every farmer knows locusts eat everything and anything. Then, as if that's not enough, you and your family get sick. Basically, God is reminding them that when they lose their livelihood, their ability to take care of themselves, when they lose their savings, their retirement which they were saving for a rainy day, which was their ability to protect themselves from unforeseen hazards of life, and when they lose their health—when all these tragedies occur, God says "if...."

God is very interesting; just when we think we have him figured out, he throws us a curveball. And it is so easy to miss these small, little features if we aren't careful. God makes an "if....then" statement. You know what we call that? It's called a conditional statement. "But wait a minute!" You might say, "God's says his love is unconditional." It is. His love never changes, but his responses do. God gives us freedom. Freedom of our will. In essence God is telling the Israelites, "If you will....then I can." The Chronicler is reminding the people of Israel, and I think us as well, that when our plans let us down, and all of the things in our lives that we count on disappear, when our health is gone, when our savings are depleted, when our ability to provide for our families is eliminated, to the point where we have nothing left to place our confidence in other than God, when we are desperate, and dependent, no longer able to stand independent from God (which is sin), when you and I are ready to stop and realize our ever-present need for help, then God is there, ready, and willing. *If my people who are called by my name will humble themselves and pray and seek My face and turn from their wicked ways, then I will hear from Heaven, and will forgive their sin and heal their land.*

Three Things about Prayer

So, what does this mean for us? First, I think the humbling, the turning, the seeking, and the recognition of our utter dependence on God for all things, even our very being, are all accomplished in the very act of prayer. We come to God easily and readily when we realize he is the source of life and the power we need to live and move and have our being. Prayer is the ultimate recognition of the sufficiency of God to meet all of our insufficiency. And when we pray to an all sufficient God, we are praying to him as he is. This means to pray "in his name" which is to say we are praying to the person, the only person, the rightful person, who has the means at his disposal to meet our dependent condition. Thus, the very requirement for engaging in prayer is to assume the position and posture of the dependent condition. And that is what a loving and merciful God requires in order to gently move in us without destroying our will and personhood.

This is the key second point. God works with us in relationship, not dictatorship. And prayer is the means through which we bring our lives, our requests, our dreams, our fears before an omnipotent and endlessly loving God to discuss, learn, pursue, inspect, gain clarity, correction, and insight into our lives and responsibilities. I happen to believe that God is the sort of being who does things through prayer that he would otherwise not do if we did not ask it of him. And I also believe that the Scriptures reveal that God does not do some things he intended to do because people asked him not to do those things. Therefore, I am arguing that God desires to work in partnership with us and empower us, to be the kinds of people whom he can freely authorize to implement his ways and will throughout the world. And this is done in conversational relationship and discipleship with Jesus. These are the "if-then" kinds of endeavors. Here is another if-then statement: "If you remain in me and my words remain in you, ask whatever you wish and it will be done for you" (John 15:7).

The third point trails the second point. I suggest prayer is designed and intended to be conversational engagement, a dialog with God. Yes, dialog—hearing directly from God, as the primary means through which we learn of him, how he teaches us, and the means through which we grow as disciples who have a mind and will that can be trusted to wield the kind of power Jesus is suggesting is available through him. I want to argue there is nothing in the canon of Scripture that eliminates the idea that God is willing and able to talk to ordinary people who desire to hear his voice and obey his guidance. This is something we can be trained and developed to do if we want to. The idea that the closing of the Bible, or the genesis of the church, has in some way mandated that God can only speak through others or Scripture is actually not supported by the facts revealed in the Scripture itself. God has, and does talk to people, today, unmediated. Now, you may not want that. And if you don't, then God is the kind of person who would know you don't want that and would likely respect your wishes. It may also be that you want God to speak something specific to you. And he may not be that kind of person or speak that way, or speak those kinds of ideas or thoughts. In short, God may not be or believe what you want or expect him to be or believe. And therefore, if you or I want a specific answer or request to come to fruition more than we want God to be God, well, then there is not much he can do with us in that situation other than let us be alone with our desires. This is why Jesus was wise enough to pray in the garden of Gethsemane: "This is what I want, but not my will, yours be done" (Luke 22:42, paraphrase).

See, when we ask God to talk to us, we have to let loose of our expectations of what he's going to say or do. And that, for some, is a very risky proposition because there is often a lack of confidence that allowing God to be God is a good thing. And we have to work through that. We may also want to admit that we can often develop or even nurture a fear that if we do hear from God, and he asks us to do something we do not want to do, we are then accountable and knowledgeable of our disobedience.

But we can begin a process of desiring to hear from and commune with God, by imagining the kind of existence or life where what we ask, in Jesus' name or according to his power and desire, is done. Can you imagine that? Where everything we ask is good, and holy, and beneficial, and creative, and loving, and best? Our imaginations are not something we use only when we read science fiction or pull out our watercolor sets. Can you imagine today what it would be like to hear God speak to you? That is not an unreasonable goal. That is our opportunity. It sort of changes our idea of prayer time, doesn't it? It's not just something we do at meals or before bedtime. It's something that Paul realized would and should be continual, or unceasing, if we realize that the God of the universe is on speed dial.

I also want to ask you, if you are not praying or don't believe in prayer, or perhaps you don't want to hear the voice of God....why? What happened? Is there a wound? Did you not get what you wanted from your prayers? Do you feel God doesn't listen to you, and you are neglected or abandoned? Why do you think that? Can you risk talking to God about your problem with God?

Conclusion

In closing, I want to suggest that you take the chance to pray silently to God. Bring him your ideas, your hopes, your requests, your anxieties, your disappointments, your confessions, whatever is right at the tip of your tongue, and talk to him. And then listen for him to talk back. You might be surprised.

Setting oneself and one's mind and thoughts on God is one of the most holy things we can ever do. We set ourselves apart. We set our minds and wills on God and his action with us in our world when we pray. And the peace of God, which transcends the realities of our daily physical limitations and difficulties, creates a hedge of protection around our hearts and minds.

Why? Because the God of the universe is in contact and communion with us through prayer. This is the power sharing arrangement of the universe. Prayer is the primary means through which God governs and directs his Kingdom and its citizens. Thus prayer has the potential to not only revolutionize our lives and perspectives for our purposes here on earth, but gives us a window into the grand purposes God has designed for all creation throughout eternity.

Truly, our Father, who is in the heavens, has a name, a character that is hallowed. May his Kingdom come, and will be done, in my life and throughout the entire universe. In prayer we move toward that reality.

Amen and Amen.

Part 6

Social Holiness

Sermon 17

Loving My Neighbor

Deborah Hearn-Chung Gin

[B]ut you shall love your neighbor as yourself: I am the Lord... you shall love the alien as yourself... I am the Lord your God (Leviticus 19:18, 34, NRSV).

What does it mean to "love your neighbor as yourself?" Or what does it mean to "love *my* neighbor as *my*self?" This command finds its origin in Leviticus 19, buried in a long list of ways God's people are to be holy, as the Lord God is holy. But for today's Christian believer, it is known as the greatest of commandments. We are familiar with Jesus' reframing of it to elevate the command to "greatest" status; Luke's version states it this way, "You shall love the Lord your God with all your heart, and with all your soul, and with all your strength, and with all your mind; and your neighbor as yourself" (Luke 10:27). Mark's and Matthew's gospels contain parallel passages.

We are, perhaps, less familiar with the fact that Jesus' exhortation gets retold in the next generation of believers in the early church. We are less familiar that this second half of the greatest commandment can be found also in the New Testament letters, for example, in Romans 13, Galatians 5, and James 2. The version in Romans urges, "Owe no one anything, except to love one another; for the one who loves another has fulfilled the law. The commandments, 'You shall not commit adultery; you shall not murder; you shall not steal; you shall not covet'; and any other commandment, are summed up in this word,

'Love your neighbor as yourself'. Love does no wrong to a neighbor; therefore, love is the fulfilling of the law" (Romans 13:8-10). The fact that the command went through three iterations points to its importance and to its centrality as a biblical message.

While the exact Levitical quote is not found in the book, the actions of two characters in the Ruth story embody what it means to love our neighbors. Let us turn now to this story to discover what God tells us about loving our neighbor. Ruth 2:8-10 reads:

> Then Boaz said to Ruth, "Now listen, my daughter, do not go to glean in another field or leave this one, but keep close to my young women. Keep your eyes on the field that is being reaped, and follow behind them. I have ordered the young men not to bother you. If you get thirsty, go to the vessels and drink from what the young men have drawn." Then she fell prostrate, with her face to the ground, and said to him, "Why have I found favor in your sight, that you should take notice of me, when I am a foreigner?"

It is an odd passage to quote in a Sunday morning service. It isn't one of those pithy, packaged dictums; rather, it places us right in the middle of an ongoing story, one of Boaz and this foreigner Ruth. As a part of a story, and not a propositional statement, we must unpack it to understand its meaning and learn what loving one's neighbor entails.

In Leviticus 19:18, there are two entities: self and neighbor. Later in Leviticus 19, the command is restated more specifically as an instruction to love "the alien" as oneself because the Israelites too were aliens in Egypt (v. 34). So, in the story of Boaz and Ruth, these two entities are Boaz (self) and Ruth (neighbor, or alien). Let us consider, then, what each does in this love exchange.

The Way that Boaz Loves

First, self. Boaz is introduced in Ruth 2 as a relative of Ruth's deceased father-in-law, Elimelech. The text in verse 1 describes him as rich and prominent. We also know that under his employ are servants (vv. 13, 21), supervisors (vv. 5, 6), reapers (vv. 4, 7, etc.), young women (vv. 8, 22, 23), and young men (vv. 9, 15). He is an Israelite man in a patriarchal society, and the text in 3:10 indicates he is not young. All of this suggests that Boaz wields at least a moderate degree of power in his community, possibly more.

What does Boaz do in his act of holy love toward the foreigner Ruth? In the passage, we see that he demonstrates love in a variety of ways. Look first at Ruth 2:8. Boaz instructs Ruth, "Do not go to glean in another field or leave this one, but keep close to my young women." Boaz' directive to stay in his field is an act of material provision for Ruth. Levitical law made such material provision available for the poor and the alien (Leviticus 19:10), and as an honorable Israelite, Boaz follows the command.

Boaz also exhibits love toward neighbor/alien with protection. The text states in Ruth 2:9 that Boaz has "ordered the young men not to bother" Ruth. As a foreigner and widow, she ranks lowest in Israel's societal structure. Deuteronomy 16, for example, charges the community of God entering the new land to keep certain festivals, and provides a listing of who shall participate: "you and your sons and your daughters, your male and female slaves, the Levites resident in your towns, as well as the *strangers*, the orphans, and the *widows* who are among you" (vs. 11). Note that Ruth is both stranger and widow, thus occupying positions last in this list. Protection for her well-being would need to be intentional. Boaz provides such protection, and in so doing, models love toward the alien Ruth.

These two ways of loving neighbor or alien are what typically come to mind when we consider Jesus' interpretation of the law: material provision and protection. When committing to love as an act of social holiness or justice, most of us would take on tasks of feeding or clothing the poor or homeless, or of volunteering at a shelter for victims of abuse. These are absolutely needed and noble deeds of love. There are additional ways that Boaz demonstrates love, however, in Ruth 2:8-10. Let us take another look.

In the last part of Ruth 2:9, note that Boaz encourages Ruth to "go to the vessels and drink from what the young men have drawn." At first glimpse, this appears to be additional material provision, and it is. However, there is more. In this one sentence, Boaz has given Ruth *access*. Commentaries suggest that such refreshment was reserved only for the reapers; those gleaning from behind were not allowed to partake. What was once off-limits to Ruth has been made open to her by one word from Boaz; he tells her to go and drink.

With this one word, Boaz also gives her *authority*. Not only can she go and drink, but she also now has the right to what others have labored over, the liquid refreshment that the men have drawn. Ruth 2:15 shows that Boaz directed his workers to "let her glean," giving her direct permission to glean among the sheaves. So, in these acts of loving his neighbor, Boaz uses his social power to provide access and authority to the alien who had no access, no authority, no social power.

How Can We Love Like Boaz?

Not many of us will be gleaning in wheat fields soon. So what might this look like in today's white-collar, blue-collar, and other-collared world? How can we love our neighbor like Boaz did for the foreigner Ruth? In order to answer this, we need a shift in perspective. We need to see Boaz with a different lens. Boaz isn't just a landowner with employees, minding his business in honorable and ethical ways. In this story, Boaz is the one with *privilege*; whether he flaunts it or acknowledges it, he is part of the dominant culture and has power. He is male, elder, and an Ephrathite of Judah. Though the land had experienced a recent economic downturn (via famine, as we see in 1:1), Boaz' wealth was robust enough to sustain his holdings through the recession, and he was now experiencing a bumper crop.

Though most of us may not have the kind of wealth that Boaz seems to have, we each enjoy multiple privileges, in various contexts, and many of us are part of the dominant group in our primary social context. So what does loving our neighbor look like for us? Material provision, as mentioned earlier, can come in the form donations to soup kitchens or volunteer work in rescue missions. But it can also come in the form of a frame shift: What if we each took a moment to recognize our wealth? What if we took a moment to own up to our wealth? If we thought of ourselves as being among the rich, then perhaps we wouldn't be so quick to want the "best deal" on the newest purchase or want to bargain down every price, at whose expense? If we acknowledged ourselves as being among the rich, then perhaps we'd be more apt to notice "the least of these" that Jesus names in Matthew 25?

What about protection, access, and authority? Finding ways to love through these means will come more easily when we acknowledge that we *have* these, and in abundance. We are able to purchase homes and live in neighborhoods of our choosing; we are able to get loans without being second-guessed about our pay-back power; we can walk down the street in a hoodie without someone wondering what we're up to; we have access to organizations and systems of upward mobility because of our privilege and status in society.

I enjoy many privileges: Though of Korean descent, I was born in the U.S., so I don't speak with an accent, unless, of course, you detect my "So-Cal-ese." This means I have access to circles that international students or new immigrants don't have; when I speak, I will be taken seriously by my peers, whereas those with accents won't. I am Asian American, so most expect me to be smart; my work won't be second-guessed, whereas the work of my colleagues of color may.

I am also a woman, younger-looking, and Korean American. So in certain circles, I don't enjoy privilege. In certain circles, it is my Anglo male colleagues that provide me access. In certain circles, it is my Korean male associates that provide me introduction. Several years ago, I attended a gathering of many first-generation Koreans at the church of a prominent pastor in the community. Two of my Korean male colleagues were also there, but I knew almost no one else. Though a faculty member at a prominent Christian university, I lacked the social capital and status to impose myself on strangers, particularly as a woman in this context. I had attended, hoping to interact with some of the people at the event, to explore ways to collaborate and contribute to the community's development. So I waited for the "higher-ranked" colleague to introduce me into the circle. No such introduction came. Instead, the other "lower-ranked" colleague motioned to me to follow him; unsolicited, he took me straight to the prominent pastor and explained who I was, and the connection was made! A small gesture, perhaps, in his mind, but with long-lasting outcomes. And love imparted and received, to be sure!

The Neighbor Loves as Well

We've looked at length at Boaz. What of Ruth, the other party? In this story, she is not technically "neighbor." She is "alien," but as we saw in

Leviticus 19, as well as in the context of Luke's version of the commandment, loving one's neighbor and loving the alien are parallel. So let's look more closely at this person, Ruth. In a chapter I wrote about Ruth in a book entitled *Mirrored Reflections: Reframing Biblical Characters*, I said:

> As a Moabite woman, Ruth comes from a line of women who, from Israel's perspective, are assertive and take initiative. Just as Lot's daughter took initiative to continue her father's lineage, so too the women of Moab invited the men of Israel into sexual immorality and worship of Baal and thereby brought a plague on Israel that killed 24,000 (Numbers 25).

What part does the neighbor or alien play in the exchange of love? Is the neighbor just a passive recipient? Does the alien merely accept the generous paternalism offered by the giver? Let us consider, now, the role of the neighbor.

We saw earlier that Ruth makes her way into Israel associated with a widow, she herself a widow, the category that is last in lists of biblical social castes. Additionally, in the book of Ruth, we learn that of the twelve references to her name, the author linked six of these with 'Moabite' (1:4, 22; 2:2, 21; 4:5, 10). She is identified as foreigner throughout the story. In this, she is portrayed as the one without power.

We must additionally recognize, however, that Ruth also loves, as alien (or neighbor). First, she demonstrates love towards Naomi in a selfless act of loyalty by committing to follow her mother-in-law back to a land foreign to Ruth, identifying with her mother-in-law's nation and God, and taking an oath of permanent daughtership. (Recall her passionate promise: "Where you go, I will go; ...your people shall be my people, and your God my God"—Ruth 1:16.)

Ruth's love toward Naomi is obvious and genuine. However, there is another layer of love in this commitment. Ruth also loves by *choosing* to follow and identify with Naomi: Ruth takes the initiative. So, while loyalty is the first, and most visible, level of love imparted by Ruth, deciding and *initiating* this sacrificial act is the deeper reflection of love.

The second way Ruth, the alien, shows love can be seen in the way she self-identifies throughout the story. Look again at Ruth 2, specifically a few verses before our initial passage. In verse 5, we read the exchange preceding Ruth and Boaz' first conversation. Boaz asks a supervisor about Ruth, referring to her as "na'arah," generic "young woman." Now watch what happens next, in the conversation between Ruth and Boaz:

> Then Boaz said to Ruth, "Now listen, my daughter, do not go to glean in another field or leave this one, but keep close to my young women. Keep your eyes on the field that is being reaped, and follow behind them. I have ordered the young men not to bother you. If you get thirsty, go to the vessels and drink from what the young men have drawn." Then she fell prostrate, with her face to the ground, and said to him, "Why have I found favor in your sight, that you should take notice of me, when I am a foreigner?" But Boaz answered her, "All that you have done for your mother-in-law since the death of your husband has been fully told me, and how you left your father and mother and your native land and came to a people that you did not know before. May the Lord reward you for your deeds, and may you have a full reward from the Lord, the God of Israel, under whose wings you have come for refuge!" Then she said, "May I continue to find favor in your sight, my lord, for you have comforted me and spoken kindly to your *shiphchah* [maidservant], even though I am not one of your servants" (Ruth 2:8-13).

Ruth responds to Boaz by self-identifying first as "nokriy" ("foreigner") in v. 10, and then, after acknowledging Boaz' kindness toward her, as "shiphchah" ("maidservant") in v. 13. In the next chapter, when she surprises Boaz with her presence in the middle of the night, she refers to herself as "'amah" ("maid") in 3:9.

The significance of these three self-identifications, in this sequence, can be seen as we consider social status. In Boaz' presence, she initially refers to herself in the lowest form, foreigner. In the same conversation, she elevates the status of her self-identification, to maidservant, but only when she saw that his generosity was specific towards her. Then, finally, she once again elevates her self-reference, to maid, after she had spent some time gleaning in his field. Yet, even though she steadily promotes her status, Ruth always keeps her self-identification lower than Boaz' address of her, as young woman. In our U.S. American society, it is difficult to comprehend the depth of this act of love that Ruth bestows on Boaz. But in societies where social status is governed by hierarchy, particularly as reflected in the language of address, the understanding is clear: Ruth shows deep deference toward Boaz in her self-references. She does so as a sign of respect and making *him* feel *at ease*, not as a way to earn his grace or to manipulate the situation. In this, she is demonstrating great love towards him.

So far, we've seen how the neighbor can love, through taking initiative and deferring to others for their comfort. The third way that Ruth reveals love is by being a mentor. Turn to chapter 3, starting in verse 8. It reads:

> At midnight the man was startled, and turned over, and there, lying at his feet, was a woman! He said, "Who are you?" And she answered, "I am Ruth, your servant; spread your cloak over your 'amah [maid], for you are next-of-kin."

Some commentators consider Ruth's act of coming to lie at Boaz' feet in the middle of the night and to direct him to spread his cloak over her as a gesture of marriage proposal. Yes, similar to our current culture, an unusual event for a woman to propose to a man! Even more, in her social position as maid to Boaz, such an instructive order seems out of place. Yet, in this act, what Ruth is doing is *mentoring* Boaz to take his place in continuing the line of Elimelech and his sons. Though Boaz is the one in the dominant position of this power relationship, Ruth is the one who acts out of a courageous love to mentor *him*!

We've seen, now, that the neighbor can also love, by choosing the difficult road, by paying sacrificial respect to the other to put them at ease, and by courageously acting as instructor when the one in power is idle, hesitant, or unaware. Though often without power, the neighbor or alien is not a passive recipient. Rather, as Ruth's actions show, the neighbor or alien also loves; we just don't naturally see it as love, perhaps, because we frame the story through our own privileged perspectives.

How Can We Love Like Ruth?

Today's Ruth, as pictured in this message, is anyone who is part of the non-dominant group in a community or larger society. In U.S. society, this may be the new immigrant, the person of color, the woman, the one with a disability, the one who is trying to survive on minimum wage. How can those of us in the non-dominant group love?

Social activist and critical pedagogue, Paulo Freire, addressing the powerful elite in Brazil, spoke out against the abuses of power, including the lack of access to basic education by the masses. In his challenge he directed attention toward both those in power and those without, explaining that it is only when those without power claim their God-given power can it be considered empowerment. If power is "given" by the privileged to the marginalized, it is not empowerment (*Pedagogy of the Oppressed*). Claiming her God-given power, Ruth was able to love in her lopsided exchange with Boaz.

The road of love for those of us who are Ruth in society is not an easy one. Loving is always a difficult act, involving much sacrifice and loss. It is also necessarily creative. And, out of deference to those who tread this road, with the many costly scars, I resist prescribing what love can look like from this perspective. Perhaps you will go from here to consider ways that you also can love, through choosing to sacrifice, intentionally deferring to the other, and rising to mentor the one in power. And perhaps those of you who are among the dominant group will consider ways that the Ruths in your community *are* loving you.

Conclusion

Loving my neighbor as myself may seem simple, even if it involves sacrifice. But the story of Boaz and Ruth gives us a glimpse into the multi-layered nature of what loving in the self-and-neighbor relationship looks like. I confess I am personally not put together to gravitate naturally toward touchy-feely, people-oriented acts of love! However, when God calls me toward justice and a loving-kindness that gives voice to the voiceless and provides access and authority to those without, as well as to recognize when the powerless are also loving, I must obey. Will you?

Sermon 18

Inspirational Sayings

Rob Muthiah

Matthew 25:31-46

When I was in high school, I was into inspirational or motivational slogans—sayings and posters and that sort of thing. I can still tell you some of the sayings my coach put up on the walls of the high school wrestling room. I can also describe for you the poster that was taped to my bedroom wall with the picture of a cowboy riding a bareback bronc and these words at the bottom: hope for the best, prepare for the worst, and take what comes.

As a high schooler trying to figure out my faith, here's one of the inspirational ditties that stuck with me. It went something like this:

> God said, "Build a better world."
> I said, "The world is such a dark and scary place;
>   there's nothing I can do."
> But God in all his wisdom said, "Just build a better you!"

As a high schooler, that did something for me. It was a nugget of inspiration for me as a budding Christian to do something good for the world.

But I'm not in high school anymore. Now I'm embarrassed just to recite this little poem because I think it's so cheesy. But there are deeper problems here, too. See if you can start to figure it out:

- By some estimates, 3 million women and girls are enslaved in the sex trade today. More women and girls are shipped off to brothels on an annual basis today than there were African slaves shipped to slave plantations annually in the 18th century.—Just build a better you?
- The population of the city of Los Angeles is 3.8 million people. Almost that number of people around the world die every year from water related diseases that we know how to prevent.—Just build a better you?
- In the U.S., 1 in every 100 adults is incarcerated. Our imprisonment rate, per capita, is almost 50 percent higher than Russia and 320 percent higher than China. The reasons are complex: It's a huge moral problem for us as a culture, with no easy answers, but I'm pretty sure "Just build a better you" isn't going to get us too far.

And here's another problem. The saying doesn't match up with the words of Jesus in Matthew 25:31-46. Listen to these words that Jesus spoke:

> When the Son of Man comes in his glory, and all the angels with him, then he will sit on the throne of his glory. All the nations will be gathered before him, and he will separate people one from another as a shepherd separates the sheep from the goats, and he will put the sheep at his right hand and the goats at the left. Then the king will say to those at his right hand, "Come, you that are blessed by my Father, inherit the kingdom prepared for you from the foundation of the world; for I was hungry and you gave me food, I was thirsty and you gave me something to drink, I was a stranger and you welcomed me, I was naked and you gave me clothing, I was sick and you took care of me, I was in prison and you visited me." Then the righteous will answer him, "Lord, when was it that we saw you hungry and gave you food, or thirsty and gave you something to drink? And when

was it that we saw you a stranger and welcomed you, or naked and gave you clothing? And when was it that we saw you sick or in prison and visited you?" And the king will answer them, "Truly I tell you, just as you did it to one of the least of these who are members of my family, you did it to me." Then he will say to those at his left hand, "You that are accursed, depart from me into the eternal fire prepared for the devil and his angels; for I was hungry and you gave me no food, I was thirsty and you gave me nothing to drink, I was a stranger and you did not welcome me, naked and you did not give me clothing, sick and in prison and you did not visit me." Then they also will answer, "Lord, when was it that we saw you hungry or thirsty or a stranger or naked or sick or in prison, and did not take care of you?" Then he will answer them, "Truly I tell you, just as you did not do it to one of the least of these, you did not do it to me." And these will go away into eternal punishment, but the righteous into eternal life (NRSV).

The passage points to the eschaton, the final age. Jesus speaks of a day when all the nations and all the people of the nations will be gathered before the Son of Man, and there's this sorting process that's going to occur.

Do you remember the Sorting Hat in the Harry Potter stories? When new students arrive at Hogwarts, they take turns putting on the Sorting Hat, and the Sorting Hat tells them which one of the four houses they will be assigned to: Gryffindor, Hufflepuff, Ravenclaw, or the sinister Slytherin. Something like that is going on here in our passage, but it's about more than where you're going to spend a few years of your high school career. Deep moral judgments will be made, and a sorting will take place, but instead of being sorted into houses, people will be sorted into one of two herds: sheep and goats.

Sheep and Goats

Now, we could try to figure out the relative value of a sheep versus a goat in the agrarian culture of that day, or we could explore sheep personalities versus goat personalities, and we could try to figure out why goats always get the worst of it. You never hear of "scape-*sheep*," do you? But it doesn't take much background information or understanding of ancient agrarian life to figure out that you really want to be with the sheep!

The sheep, those who inherit the kingdom, are those who fed the hungry, gave drink to the thirsty, welcomed the stranger, clothed those who had nothing to wear, and visited those in prison. Jesus commends them for doing these things: "Truly I tell you, just as you did it to one of the least of these who are members of my family, you did it to me" (v. 40). The message to us is clear: Be this type of people!

Look at what's going on here. This is the last of several parables and stories in a row about being ready for Jesus Christ's second coming. The passage talks about a sorting of the sheep from the goats in relation to that second coming, and within it we have ethical instruction about how to live. The urgent call to be prepared for Christ's return is connected to our concrete activism in the here and now.

> Be prepared...feed the hungry.
> Be prepared...clothe those with nothing to wear.
> Be prepared...visit those in prison.

Jesus is setting forth a Christian spirituality that is not other-worldly, but that is connected to suffering brothers and sisters in *this* world.

Here we get to the problem with the little poem about "just build a better you." As Jesus sets forth these ethical instructions in Matt. 25, he has an awful lot to say about what you are supposed to do for people who are *not* you. Feed people who are *not* you. Give water to thirsty people who are *not* you. Clothe and attend to the medical needs of people who are *not* you. Disciples of Christ have a faith that leads them into these kind of activities directed at *others*, directed at people who are *not you*.

"Just build a better you" is a solution drenched in individualism. It emerges from a line of thinking that says, if everyone focuses on *themselves* and everyone improves *themselves*, then everything will work out, and the world will be a beautiful place. Jesus challenges this sort of individualism. I don't think he lets us off the hook when it comes to personal responsibility, but he calls his disciples to go *beyond* the logic of personal responsibility and personal self-improvement to embrace the logic of the kingdom that reaches out to others in need, a logic that involves mutuality, a caring for each other, and an extending of oneself to others.

Taking Holiness Seriously

Azusa Pacific University, where I teach, identifies with the Wesleyan tradition, a tradition that takes holiness seriously. One version of what it means to be holy goes like this: If you want to be holy, then you need to have your daily quiet time, make sure you've asked forgiveness for any impure thoughts you've had, and don't say any cuss words. These are good practices and I commend them to you. But if that's the sum of what we think it means to be holy, then we haven't listened to the words of Jesus.

Holiness involves being the type of people who are fit to be in the presence of God, and here in Matthew 25, Jesus says that this kind of people are the people who are actively living out their faith by meeting the needs of others. Being fit for the kingdom of God involves much more than a few personal spiritual practices. It means caring for our brothers and sisters in need.

And Jesus says, "just as you did it to one of the least of these who are members of my family, you did it to me."

Let me tell you some stories of what this looks like. A few years ago a woman who is a member of Foothill Community Church came to the pastor with an idea. She wanted to start serving one meal a week to the homeless in Azusa. With her inspiration and the help of others, the first meal was prepared and served. Now several years later, every Saturday afternoon you can still go over to Foothill Community Church and get a free meal or volunteer to help prepare and serve a meal for our brothers and sisters in need.

And Jesus says, "just as you did it to one of the least of these who are members of my family, you did it to me."

Not long ago volunteers were needed in Pasadena where I live to help conduct a homeless survey. Doing a homeless census is necessary for getting government funding for programs to assist these people. But this particular survey was also important because it sought to identify the most at-risk of the homeless in order to provide them with comprehensive assistance—medical, psychological, housing, veteran's benefits—a focused effort to help those who were most at risk of dying on the streets. Did you know that the best time to conduct these kinds of surveys is early in the morning—like at 5 a.m.? I didn't know that. Volunteers met at a church before 5 a.m., picked up their surveys, and were assigned a few blocks to canvas. You find people sleeping on stair landings and in the bushes behind stores. Wake them up; ask them the necessary questions; and then give them a coupon for food. A couple people from my church chose to get up at this early hour of the morning two days in a row to help out because they saw it as a way to engage in the actions called for in Matthew 25.

And Jesus says, "just as you did it to one of the least of these who are members of my family, you did it to me."

If we care about people who are struggling, then we should also care about programs and policies that can help—or hurt—these same people. Food for the Hungry is one organization that is doing wonderful things on the bigger program level. In Mozambique, Food for the Hungry workers have taught farmers new techniques regarding plant density, preserving produce, and improving the soil. These trained farmers have then taught other local farmers. As a result, these families have increased food security and income. Food for the Hungry is doing similar work in countries like Burundi, Indonesia, and Bolivia. We can get involved by making financial donations to support the work of Food for the Hungry or similar organizations. Writing a check is not as hands-on as volunteering to serve a meal, but it all works together. Our financial involvment makes a big difference in addressing issues of hunger and poverty.

And Jesus says, "just as you did it to one of the least of these who are members of my family, you did it to me."

A friend of mine, David, works for an organization called Bread for the World. It's a non-partisan, Christian organization that works to get Congress to pass legislation that will address issues of hunger both domestically and internationally. Bread for the World promotes legislation that funds things like child nutrition programs for kids here in the U.S., where one in five children live in households that struggle to put food on the table. Bread for the World also seeks to get legislation passed that will direct U.S. foreign aid to the programs that are most effective in addressing hunger locally. Check out its website for more details. Some years my local church has been part of a letter writing campaign organized by Bread for the World. We would gather around tables after church and write letters to our members of Congress and the President, asking them to support specific legislation that will address hunger and letting them know that we think reducing hunger is hugely important. Thoughtful, personally written letters have a big influence on our elected officials. It's a way we can seek to address hunger on the policy level. Writing letters to elected officials is not very glamorous work, but it makes a difference. It is a concrete way of living out the values of Matthew 25.

And Jesus says, *"just as you did it to one of the least of these who are members of my family, you did it to me."*

Values of Matthew 25

Do you ever find yourself inspired by examples like these, but then a few moments later immobilized and depressed? I mean, there's *so much to do*. Do I start helping with a tutoring program at our local school, or do I serve more meals at the homeless shelter, or do I quit my job to work with the poor overseas...but what about the poor here at home?

It can feel so overwhelming. I can feel stuck. And those feelings of being overwhelmed and stuck aren't fun. That feeling of stuckness—I've had nightmares about being a student and getting half way through the term and realizing I was registered for an additional class, and I hadn't attended it even once; it was a math class, and if you didn't get the earlier concepts, then there was no way you could understand the newer formulas; there was an exam scheduled for tomorrow, and I couldn't possible be ready and...in the haze of semi-consciousness, I try to tell myself it's not real. Or the running-but-unable-to-move dream? Trapped, overwhelmed, stuck. Do you ever feel that way? Maybe even when you're not dreaming?

Sometimes I can read Matthew 25 and feel that way. There are so many poor and hungry people. There are so many issues that contribute to the fact that 16,000 children around the world will die today because they didn't have enough to eat. It overwhelms and depresses me that in our own country, where one in four kids is at risk of hunger, half the produce we grow in this country ends up being thrown away. The scope can be crushing.

When our *inspiration* has turned into *desperation*, how do we move on to *actualization*? How do we move on to make things happen on behalf of the least of these?

First of all, you don't have to do it on your own. If you look around, it doesn't take long to see that there's a lot already going on. If you open your eyes, then you'll see them: people who are making inconvenient choices to reach out to the least of these. I know some office staff at a local public school who on their own took a girl to the store and bought her a dress so that she had something to wear to the 8th grade graduation because her family couldn't afford it. I know a woman who leads trips to Peru as part of efforts to dig wells so villagers can have clean drinking water. An older gentleman I know coordinates his church's collection of canned goods for a local food bank. These people are not taking on the whole world, but they're doing something. They're taking on a little piece, and taking on a little piece doesn't seem so overwhelming to me. I realize that I don't have to try to take on all the world's problems on my own.

Another thing that helps me get unstuck is remembering that I don't have to start something new. I don't know how to start a relief and development organization or a homeless shelter, but that's ok. I can jump in with others who are already up and running. My denomination was coordinating relief kits for Iraqi refugees, and my church bought supplies and assembled kits to be combined with kits from a bunch of other churches and shipped to Iraq. We didn't have to invent the program. What is your denomination or churches in your area doing that you can partner with? You can also get on the internet and learn more about how you can partner with Food for the Hungry, Bread for the World, or the many other good organizations doing this work. Find partners. You don't have to take on all the problems by yourself, and you don't have to start something new. As I remind myself of these two thoughts, the way forward appears more possible.

Conclusion

I want to close with a story from the South African novelist, Alan Paton, who wrote a book titled *Ah, But Your Land Is Beautiful*. In it we meet a man named Mr. Mansfield who is the principal at a school for whites. His superiors have ordered him to cancel a cricket match he scheduled between his school and the cricket team from a black school. Mr. Mansfield is so committed to tearing down the things that keep whites and blacks apart that he decides to resign from his job rather than carry out the order. A man named Mr. Nene, a black man, comes to his office to talk with him. They talk about the political struggles against apartheid, and in the course of their conversation, Mr. Nene talks about how they are both going to be wounded because they both are committed to fighting against the injustices around them. They're both going to be wounded. And then as he rises to leave, Mr. Nene says in a cheerful voice, "I don't worry about the wounds. When I go up there, which is my intention, the Big Judge will say to me, Where are your wounds? and if I say I haven't any, he will say, Was there nothing to fight for? I couldn't face that question."

Where are your wounds? Was there nothing to fight for?

My brothers and sisters in Christ, there *are* things worth fighting for. There are families that are dying of hunger in a world where there is enough. Men and women and children are dying of preventable diseases because of economic choices the rest of us make...or are unwilling to make. There are 1.5 billion people trying to live on less than $1.25 a day. Jesus connected the way we act on behalf of these people to the sorting of sheep and goats at his second coming. In Matthew 25, he gives us a clear picture of how we are to be living as we await the fullness of the kingdom of God. May the Holy Spirit transform our lethargy and anxiety into cheerful action and hope for the future, and may we boldly reach out to our brothers and sisters in need.

And Jesus says, "just as you did it to one of the least of these who are members of my family, you did it to me."

Sermon 19

Violence and Passivity vs. Jesus' Third Way

Paul Alexander

You've heard that it was said, "Eye for eye, and tooth for tooth." But I tell you, don't resist an evil person with evil. If someone strikes you on the right cheek, turn to him the other also. And if someone wants to sue you and take your tunic, let him have your cloak as well. If someone forces you to go one mile, go with him two miles. Give to the one who asks you, and do not turn away from the one who wants to borrow from you. You've heard that it was said, "Love your neighbor and hate your enemy." But I tell you: love your enemies and pray for those who persecute you (Matthew 5:38-45, NASB & Author's Translation).

Imagine life in early first century Palestine. Taxes are exorbitant; guerilla warfare is always a possibility; and Roman occupational forces crucify revolutionaries and their families by the hundreds, sometimes thousands. This is the terrifying reality of Jesus' life.

Despite hundreds of years of a tradition of retributive "justice" like Cain's sevenfold retribution and Lamech's seventy-sevenfold retribution, and even the then-revolutionary Mosaic "eye for eye and tooth for tooth," Jesus taught and the early church repeated, "do not violently resist evil. If someone strikes you on the right cheek, turn to them the other also." I imagine Palestinians living under occupation forces probably responded to that command with a hearty "What the heck?!?"

In teaching to turn the other cheek, Jesus offered a possibility beyond the instinctual "fight or flight" responses. Jesus offered a third way, a way that requires intention, that moves beyond a visceral reaction and into the determined space that precedes reconciliation. Jesus said to turn the *other* cheek. Turning the *other* cheek is not passive; it requires people to stand their ground and not to leave. Jesus' teaching embodies holiness, which emphasizes justice as well as love, advocacy as well as forgiveness, and peacemaking as well as sacrifice.

Turning the Other Cheek

Walter Wink argues that, in the domination system of the first century, a strike on the right cheek would have been a backhanded, insulting slap with the right hand. The right cheek was the cheek of insult, rejection, and inferiority. But when two self-perceived equals fought, they would strike the left cheek with a fist. The left cheek was the cheek of equality, dignity, and respect. Jesus said, if you get hit, then you're to get back up and face the oppressor with your cheek of dignity, respect, and equality. When you turn the other cheek, you face your attacker with your "made in the image of God" cheek.

This is an action. It's an action that subverts the oppressor's illusion of superiority. And by refusing to resist violence with violence, the one who is attacked also refuses to take on the role of the oppressor. The attacked one, standing there with the cheek of dignity facing forward and the cheek of indignity firmly turned away, offers the violent one new possibilities. And just like the one who was hit had three options—fight, flight, or turn the cheek—the one who hit now has three options as well. Consider the following three options:

1. The oppressors could hit the left cheek with a fist. But this would acknowledge the slave, the servant, the woman, the "inferior," as an equal. It would turn the world a bit upside down, which could be the beginning of a good thing. The internal emancipation of the oppressed—realizing their own value before God in their minds, in their hearts, in the

depths of their soul—leads to the power to work to liberate the oppressors as well. Each of their hopes for liberation lie together, and it's the action of turning the left cheek toward the oppressors that opens up the possibility of mutual liberation. If the oppressors clench their fist and deliver a bone-crunching blow to the equality cheek of the oppressed, then this one little subordinate has nonviolently affirmed their own dignity, which is also affirmed violently by the oppressors. Direct nonviolent love can elicit violence.

2. The oppressors may walk away, refusing to affirm the dignity and equality of the oppressed. This is the passive response. It's also possible that the surprising nature of the left cheek turn leaves the attackers bewildered. When the "victim" deviates from the expected public script of violence or passivity, fight or flight, the "victim" is not playing the role of victim that the oppressors expect; a crack has opened up, and God's truth is present in the world in a way it was not before the turning of that one particular left cheek (James Scott, *Hidden Transcripts*).

3. The third possibility requires some kind of faith. If there is a God, if the Holy Spirit is working in this world, and if murderers like Saul can become saints like Paul, then the third way of Jesus can make way for the third way for oppressors. Quite simply: The oppressors could repent. When the oppressors are confronted in this direct and loving way, they have the opportunity to realize their sin.

Turning the left cheek is an accusation and an invitation. Turning the left cheek creates real space and time for transformation. Turning the left cheek opens up a redemptive story line and creates the potential for enemies to become friends. Yes, it seems a little over-the-top to imagine the attackers falling to their knees in confession and repentance, but since turning the cheek is often dismissively connected with allowing an enemy to kill you, let's also include the most redemptive possibility for this story's end.

Violent oppression presents three broad story possibilities for the follower of Jesus who is hit: Resisting with violence, not resisting at all, or resisting with active love by standing and turning the cheek. Jesus teaches explicitly against the first way, does not address the second way, and explicitly teaches the third way.

Unfortunately, this phrase is usually mistranslated "do not resist evil" or "do not resist an evil person," rather than "do not violently resist with evil" or "do not resist an evil person with evil" (Clarence Jordan, *Substance of Faith*). As a result, Jesus' teaching against violent resistance has been misunderstood as supporting passivity and non-participation in resistance of any kind. But "do not be a violent revolutionary" does not mean "roll over and accept oppression and injustice." This mistranslation has had a profoundly adverse effect on understanding Jesus' teaching to resist evil lovingly and to overcome evil with good.

Responding to Economic Exploitation

In addition to teaching a third way to respond to violence, Jesus taught a third way to resist and respond nonviolently to economic exploitation. "When someone sues you for your outer garment, give them your undergarment as well." This is yet another seemingly absurd teaching of Jesus. What are we supposed to do when our enemies take practically our last remaining shred of clothing and dignity? Give them more!

Picture an ancient courtroom with judges, witnesses, prosecutors, observers, and an accused (either male or female), who is the poorest of the poor. Imagine he's a *campesino* (or peasant) who's lost his land because of imperial policy that consolidates land in the hands of the few (the richest 1% ruled the roost in Jesus' day, too). So, a person with no land, no assets, and no money is being sued for his shirt to make sure that he repays debt incurred as a result of unjust policies. All he has is his clothes and his body. When the judge says that the poor person is to give his outer garment to the creditor, Jesus suggests that he should strip of all his clothes and stand there completely naked in the courtroom. Here's the thing: nakedness doesn't shame the poor person as much as it shames the people who cause it to happen—the one suing as well as the system that allowed (and continues to allow) such an atrocity to happen. Humiliating oneself humiliated the oppressors.

This is a third way of dealing with economic exploitation and abuse that is neither violent nor passive. Rather than breaking the kneecaps of the creditor or throwing up your hands, since "you can't fight City Hall," Jesus instead taught a prophetic, nonviolent, and active way to respond to economic oppression and injustice that empowers the disenfranchised. Jesus said that when someone seeks to exploit you economically, take off all your clothes in public. You know what's really naked then? The oppressor's self-interest.

Going God's Second Mile

What would it be like to live in a homeland occupied by a foreign military that claims to be bringing you peace? You have to work from dawn until dusk just to try to feed your family and pay tax collectors who keep as much as they can and pass the rest up the chain of command to the foreign power. What would it be like to have one of those soldiers drag you away from *your* work and make you do *his* work? When a soldier pulls a carpenter away from his craft, the carpenter has to quit working, carry the pack as far as the soldier says, and then walk all the way back to his shop. It could waste half a day or more. At the end of the mile (or more), there are two standard ways that a commandeered peasant could respond to the soldier, and of course there is Jesus' third way.

First, the person could drop or throw down the pack, run a ways back, pick up some rocks, shout, and flip him the first century version of the middle finger. Or maybe the occupying soldier picked a Jewish revolutionary who carried a curved dagger and trained for the opportunity to kill Roman soldiers and Jewish "collaborators." Some of Jesus' own disciples were revolutionaries; there were likely many more in his audiences, and folks who were not revolutionaries themselves certainly had friends or relatives who were.

A second realistic possibility at the end of that first mile is passive: to lay down the pack and walk back home. The soldier did what he could legally do; the peasant did what he was told to do, and the status quo remains unchallenged and unchanged. Sometimes acceptance of oppression and injustice seems like the wisest way to survive.

But Jesus always has a third way, one that is not violent, and is not passive. Jesus said to carry the enemy's pack an additional mile. Not one, but two. After the soldier diverts the peasant, the fisherman, or the carpenter from their work for an afternoon, they are told by Jesus to give more time, more energy, and more space to this enemy. I think we have to ask what Jesus expected during that second mile. The first mile belonged to the Empire of Rome, to the oppressor, to the soldier. It was demanded forcefully. The second mile belongs to the Empire of God, to the oppressed, to the peasant. It is given freely, and it is God's mile.

Jesus doesn't tell us in this passage what to do during the second mile, but we can get it from his other teachings. Jesus told his disciples to drop their gifts to God and go work for reconciliation when they realized there was offense between them and someone else. Jesus also told his followers to give food and drink to their enemies. So I imagine that during that second mile, Jesus hoped his followers would put his teachings into practice. I imagine Jesus wanted his followers to engage in conversation with the soldier. Perhaps a conversation could go like this, "How long have you been stationed in Palestine?" "A little over three years." "Do you have any family?" "Yeah, I have a wife and three kids." "Have you been able to get home to see them at all?" "No, and I don't get to head back for another two years." "Where are you from?" "Tuscany." "Oh, do you get much good home cooking?" "Not at all; they don't like us around here too much, and put stuff in our food that gives us diarrhea." "Well, how about you come over to our place, and we'll make you some good hummus and falafel and feed you right. We'll eat out of the same bowls and share the same bread so you'll know it's good."

I think this point might be another "Say what?!?" moment for Jesus' listeners. And the moment includes the hope that the occupation soldier from Italy would begin to follow Jesus and become a disciple too. Walking with that particular soldier for that particular extra mile includes that soldier in the love of God, flips the script of dominion, and humanizes soldier and peasant.

If discipleship includes teaching what Jesus taught then when a Roman soldier, or anyone else, starts to become a follower of Jesus and enters into the journey of discipleship, then they ought to be taught to become people who love their enemies. They ought to turn their cheeks, carry occupiers' packs, and give their underwear when sued (Peter Ellis, *Matthew: His Mind and His Message*).

Conclusion

When Jesus said, "Blessed are the peacemakers, for they are the children of God," I think these ways of being and living are what he was talking about. Peacemaking advances God's love and justice, holiness and salvation. When followers of Jesus work through the hardest parts of life in a third way, they act like God's children. It's a peacemaking that refuses to acquiesce to the status quo or fight oppression with violence. It makes something new. It makes a new world.

Epilogue
No Holiness But Social Holiness

Don Thorsen

In the Preface to his first edition of *Hymns and Sacred Poems* (1739), John Wesley famously said that there is "no holiness but social holiness." The primary meaning he had for this claim is that holiness ordinarily begins and grows in the context of being with other likeminded believers, for whom God is the highest priority in their lives. Of course, people initially become holy when they convert in response to the gospel message of Jesus Christ. Through the ongoing presence and work of the Holy Spirit, Christians believe that Jesus' death and resurrection make people holy—not by their own merits, but through Jesus who by grace fulfills all God's requirements for our salvation.

Just as Wesley's words can be understood primarily in terms of becoming holy through conversion and subsequent growth in holiness, it can also be understood in a secondary way. For Wesley, holiness applied to how you relate in every way to others. This holism not only includes how you relate with others individually, but how you relate with them collectively, publicly, and civically. With this understanding, *social holiness* applies to how you relate with others physically as well as spiritually, individually as well as collectively, justly as well as lovingly.

Jesus exemplified this social holiness in his own life and ministry. Jesus announced his ministry in his hometown of Nazareth. When asked to read the weekly Scripture, Jesus chose the following words from Isaiah:

> The Spirit of the Lord is upon me, because he has anointed me to bring good news to the poor. He has sent me to proclaim release to the captives and recovery of sight to the blind, to let the

oppressed go free, to proclaim the year of the Lord's favour (Luke 4:18-19, quoting Isaiah, NRSV).

When he finished reading, Jesus said, "Today this scripture has been fulfilled in your hearing" (Luke 4:21). In addition to fulfilling prophecy, Jesus made it clear that he undertook a holistic ministry, including ongoing care for the poor as well as proclamation of the gospel—to everyone, and especially to the poor. By the gracious aid of God's Holy Spirit, Jesus set people free from that which ensnared them: hunger as well as sin, physical blindness as well as spiritual ignorance, unjust oppression as well as demonic possession.

Wesley captured this balance of ministry, found in Jesus, as well as anyone I know. Thus, I commend Wesley's well-balanced approach to ministering to others, as he reflects Jesus' example and priorities for social holiness. *Although Christians often think of holiness individualistically, the holy living to which God calls us includes both individual and social involvement because of the testimony of Scripture, especially as found in the life and ministry of Jesus.*

How Do We Grow Spiritually?

Ordinarily spiritual growth occurs through various means of grace by which God empowers and perfects people's Christ-likeness. These spiritual means, practices, or disciplines include active participation: prayer, study (especially of scripture), worship, celebration, service, and giving; they may also include self-discipline: silence, solitude, meditation, contemplation, fasting, chastity, frugality, and sacrifice. It has been my experience that Christians most often prefer spiritual practices that allow them to become more active; they want to know what they can do to contribute actively to their spirituality. But I think that they equally benefit by slowing down—by taking time to be silent and listen to God, to meditate on Scripture, and to contemplate their relationship with God and how they may better love God and others.

Although these means of grace may be done individually, Wesley thought that they were most effective when done in relationship and accountability with others. In the context of churches or small groups, Christians may advise, commiserate with, encourage, and exhort one another, when it is helpful. Wesley developed an elaborate network of small groups in order to accomplish these ministerial networks—opportunities for social holiness. For example, Wesley started midweek services, before they became popular, known as Methodist *Societies*. In addition, Wesley developed *Class-Meetings*, which consisted of a small group of participants, affording more intimacy and accountability. The smallest groups were called *Bands* (or *Select Bands*), consisting of a group of same-gender participants, and they emphasized daily communication and accountability, which contributed to holy living.

Compassion and Advocacy

Although Wesley intended the phrase social holiness to apply primarily to Christian nurture into holiness, it secondarily applies to how holiness is concerned with people's physical, social, and just well-being as well as for their spiritual, salvific, and obedient well-being. Wesley's life and ministry were filled with examples of how he balanced biblical emphases with regard to the holistic needs of people.

In talking about Wesley's care for the poor, I like to make the distinction between his *compassion ministries*, on the one hand, and *advocacy ministries*, on the other hand. Most Christians are familiar with compassion ministries; they have to do with caring for the *symptoms* of poverty. Such care may include giving money to the financially impoverished, food to the hungry and shut-ins, short-term housing for those who are homeless, Christmas gifts for children around the world, and other charitable acts. These responses to immediate needs are often met with immediate gratefulness, and everyone benefits as a result. However, the causes for people's impoverishment—of one sort or another—may remain.

Advocacy ministries are not so much concerned about the symptoms of impoverishment as they are for their *causes*. For example: Why are people poor? Why are they hungry? Why are people sick? Why have they been treated unjustly, perhaps through neglect, marginalization, oppression, or persecution? Causation, of course, is difficult to determine, and our growing awareness of the interconnectedness of problems people face makes it daunting to pinpoint their sources.

Some Christians simplistically reduce life's problems to individual sin, evil, or Satan. As such the problems of life may seem intractable, and little—this side of heaven—can be done about them. Why try? Or worse, other Christians believe that the world must come to a cataclysmic end, which only God can ultimately put right. This latter expectation actually makes some Christians giddy when famines, earthquakes, and wars occur throughout the world, since it reinforces their expectation that nothing more can be done by them socially—much less individualistically—with regard to the poor and suffering. Even if there may be a cataclysmic end to the world, Wesley did not think that Christians are absolved from acting justly, compassionately, and with advocacy here and now. Although individual sin and evil can be catastrophic, social sin and evil can be exponentially worse. As such, Christians should be equally concerned about *and* activist on behalf of alleviating the social causes of impoverishment, discrimination, and violence as well as caring for their symptoms.

Holy, Wholly Holy!

Wesley as well as Jesus challenge us today to live holy lives—lives that are wholly holy, and not reduced to a narrowly individualistic conception of holiness. To Jesus there was no distinction between individual and social holiness; they are inextricably bound up with one another. If we claim to be followers of Jesus, then we need to incorporate into our lives and ministries the kind of holiness that impacts every dimension of life: spiritually and physically, individually and corporately, ministerially and socially. If we are to love God and love others as we love ourselves (Mark 12:29-31), which is the essence of holy living, then our love should not only be for every person, but for every part of their lives.

Appendix 1

The Holiness Manifesto[1]

The Crisis We Face

There has never been a time in greater need of a compelling articulation of the message of holiness.

Pastors and church leaders at every level of the church have come to new heights of frustration in seeking ways to revitalize their congregations and denominations. What we are doing is not working. Membership in churches of all traditions has flat-lined. In many cases, churches are declining. We are not even keeping pace with the biological growth rate in North America. The power and health of churches has also been drained by the incessant search for a better method, a more effective fad, a newer and bigger program to yield growth. In the process of trying to lead growing, vibrant churches, our people have become largely ineffective and fallen prey to a generic Christianity that results in congregations that are indistinguishable from the culture around them. Churches need a clear, compelling message that will replace the 'holy grail' of methods as the focus of our mission!

---

[1] "The Holiness Manifesto" is a convergence document completed by participants in the Wesleyan Holiness Study Project, after four years of consultations, at Azusa Pacific University in Azusa, California, 2006. The document was published by Kevin W. Mannoia and Don Thorsen, eds., *The Holiness Manifesto* (Grand Rapids: Eerdmans, 2008), 18-21. "The Holiness Manifesto" may also be found online in the Chinese, Korean, and Spanish languages on the Wesleyan Holiness Consortium website, *http://www.holinessandunity.org/index.php/resources* (accessed October 4, 2013).

Many church leaders have become hostages to the success mentality of numeric and programmatic influence. They have become so concerned about 'how' they do church that they have neglected the weightier matter of 'what' the church declares. We have inundated the 'market' with methodological efforts to grow the church. In the process, many of our leaders have lost the ability to lead. They cannot lead because they have no compelling message to give, no compelling vision of God, no transformational understanding of God's otherness. They know it and long to find the centering power of a message that makes a difference. Now more than ever, they long to soak up a deep understanding of God's call to holiness—transformed living. They want a mission. They want a message!

People all around are looking for a future without possessing a spiritual memory. They beg for a generous and integrative word from Christians that makes sense and makes a difference. If God is going to be relevant to people, we have a responsibility to make it clear to them. We have to shed our obsession with cumbersome language, awkward expectations, and intransigent patterns. What is the core, the center, the essence of God's call? That is our message, and that is our mission!

People in churches are tired of our petty lines of demarcation that artificially create compartments, denominations, and divisions. They are tired of building institutions. They long for a clear, articulate message that transcends institutionalism and in-fighting among followers of Jesus Christ. They are embarrassed by the corporate mentality of churches that defend parts of the gospel as if it were their own. They want to know the unifying power of God that transforms. They want to see the awesomeness of God's holiness that compels us to oneness in which there is a testimony of power. They accept the fact that not all of us will look alike; there will be diversity. But they want to know that churches and leaders believe that we are one—bound by the holy character of God who gives us all life and love. They want a message that is unifying. The only message that can do that comes from the nature of God, who is unity in diversity.

Therefore, in this critical time, we set forth for the church's well being a fresh focus on holiness. In our view, this focus is the heart of scripture concerning Christian existence for all times—and clearly for our time.

The Message We Have

God is holy and calls us to be a holy people.

God, who is holy, has abundant and steadfast love for us. God's holy love is revealed to us in the life and teachings, death and resurrection of Jesus Christ, our Savior and Lord. God continues to work, giving life, hope and salvation through the indwelling of the Holy Spirit, drawing us into God's own holy, loving life. God transforms us, delivering us from sin, idolatry, bondage, and self-centeredness to love and serve God, others, and to be stewards of creation. Thus, we are renewed in the image of God as revealed in Jesus Christ.

Apart from God, no one is holy. Holy people are set apart for God's purpose in the world. Empowered by the Holy Spirit, holy people live and love like Jesus Christ. Holiness is both gift and response, renewing and transforming, personal and communal, ethical and missional. The holy people of God follow Jesus Christ in engaging all the cultures of the world and drawing all peoples to God.

Holy people are not legalistic or judgmental. They do not pursue an exclusive, private state of being better than others. Holiness is not flawlessness but the fulfillment of God's intention for us. The pursuit of holiness can never cease because love can never be exhausted.

God wants us to be, think, speak, and act in the world in a Christ-like manner. We invite all to embrace God's call to:

- be filled with all the fullness of God in Jesus Christ—Holy Spirit-endowed co-workers for the reign of God;
- live lives that are devout, pure, and reconciled, thereby being Jesus Christ's agents of transformation in the world;
- live as a faithful covenant people, building accountable community, growing up into Jesus Christ, embodying the spirit of God's law in holy love;
- exercise for the common good an effective array of ministries and callings, according to the diversity of the gifts of the Holy Spirit;

- practice compassionate ministries, solidarity with the poor, advocacy for equality, justice, reconciliation and peace; and
- care for the earth, God's gift in trust to us, working in faith, hope, and confidence for the healing and care of all creation.

By the grace of God, let us covenant together to be a holy people.

The Action We Take

May this call impel us to rise to this biblical vision of Christian mission:

- Preach the transforming message of holiness;
- Teach the principles of Christ-like love and forgiveness;
- Embody lives that reflect Jesus Christ;
- Lead in engaging with the cultures of the world; and
- Partner with others to multiply its effect for the reconciliation of all things.

For this we live and labor to the glory of God.

Appendix 2

Fresh Eyes on Holiness: Living Out the Holiness Manifesto[2]

As leaders press forward in living out holiness in their ministry, the following represents themes they will need to consider carefully in future years. We offer this as an invitation to engage together in unity around the transforming message entrusted to our care.

Dimensions of Holiness

- Holiness has several dimensions: Within each dimension there are contrasting realities. It is important to embrace both elements of each contrast in order to experience and practice holiness in its completeness.
- Individual and Corporate: We are called to be holy persons individually and to be a holy people corporately. The corporate aspect of holiness which is prominent in Scripture needs to be emphasized again in this time and culture.
- Christ-centered and Holy Spirit-centered: The Holy Spirit's work within us leads to conformity to the person of

---

[2] "Fresh Eyes on Holiness: Living Out the Holiness Manifesto" is a convergence document completed by participants in the Wesleyan Holiness Study Project, at Azusa Pacific University in Azusa, California, 2007. The document was published by Kevin W. Mannoia and Don Thorsen, eds., *The Holiness Manifesto* (Grand Rapids: Eerdmans, 2008), 22-25. "Fresh Eyes on Holiness: Living Out the Holiness Manifesto" may also be found online on the Wesleyan Holiness Consortium website, *http://www.holinessandunity.org/index.php/resources/fresh-eyes-on-holiness* (accessed October 4, 2013).

Jesus Christ. Neither should be expressed without the other.

- Development and End: God has an ultimate purpose for each person, which is to be like Jesus Christ. Teaching on development in the Christian life should keep the end of Christ-likeness in view.
- Crisis and Process: A definite work of God's grace in our hearts and our ongoing cooperation to his grace are to be equally emphasized.
- Blessings and Suffering: Full union with Jesus Christ brings many blessings but also a sharing of his sufferings.
- Separation and Incarnation: Holy people are in but not of the world. Holiness requires both separation and redemptive, reconciling, and restorative engagement.
- Forms and Essence: Holiness always expresses itself in particular forms, which are the ways in which it is translated into life and action. But the forms must not be confused with the essence of holiness itself.
- How do you balance these contrasting realities in your personal life and ministry? Where do you see the need for greater balance?

Essence of Holiness

The essence of holiness is that God is holy and calls us to be a holy people. The challenge is reflecting Jesus Christ in a relevant and contextual way that transcends social location and diversity. Indwelled and empowered by the Holy Spirit, holy people live and love like Jesus Christ. Walking intimately with him overflows in compassion and advocacy for those whom God loves.

How can you effectively embody holiness in the context where you are now, personally and in ministry?

Catholicity of Holiness

Although differences have led to fragmentation in churches, holiness invites unity. God wants to heal—to make whole—the brokenness of people, churches, and society. The impact of holiness goes beyond boundaries of tradition, theology, gender, ethnicity, and time to affect people and institutional structures. The resulting healing unites all Christians in wholeness, growing up into Christ-likeness. The message of holiness involves conversation and engagement with others.

What conversations and actions do you need to engage in to bring healing to people, churches, and society?

Holiness and Culture

Holiness people, while themselves influenced by culture, must convey the holiness message within multiple cultures. Culture affects the holiness message and churches because we are socially shaped human beings. Culture challenges us to mediate holiness in ways that are relevant and transforming without losing the integrity of the message.

How do we exegete culture and subculture in order to achieve transformation? How might you embody the holiness message in your immediate pastoral setting?

Holiness and Community

Individual and corporate holiness require that faith communities pursue organizational structures, processes, and content that promote radical obedience to Jesus Christ. Holiness does not develop in isolation from other believers and faith communities that provide spiritual support and accountability.

What communal structures, processes, and content would help promote radical obedience to Jesus Christ, personally and in ministry?

Holiness and Social Concern

Social engagement is an essential incarnational expression of personal and social holiness. It includes ministry among the poor, disenfranchised, and marginalized. Holiness requires a response to the world's deepest and starkest needs. Social engagement is the continuing work of Jesus Christ in and through the church by the Holy Spirit for the world.

Since proclamation of the gospel of Jesus Christ to the poor is essential, how do you embody the continuing personal and social engagement with the disenfranchised and marginalized?

Communicating Holiness

Christians live in environments of changing language. They must communicate a holiness message in ways that are clear, relevant, and winsome. The message of holiness often has been communicated with terms and paradigms that are not understood today.

What terms and paradigms could you use to communicate the holiness message in a compelling way?

List of Contributors

Paul Alexander, Ph.D., is Professor of Christian Ethics and Public Policy at Palmer Theological Seminary. While at the Azusa Pacific Graduate School of Theology, Dr. Alexander was Professor of Theology and Ethics, and Director of the Doctor of Ministry Program.

Tony Baron, D.Min., Psy.D., is Associate Professor of Christian Leadership in the Azusa Pacific Graduate School of Theology, and Director of the Graduate School of Theology in San Diego.

Gary Black, Jr., Ph.D., is Associate Professor in the Azusa Pacific Graduate School of Theology, Chair of the Department of Advanced Studies, and Director of the Doctor of Ministry Program.

T. Scott Daniels, Ph.D., is Dean of the Azusa Pacific Graduate School of Theology, and Professor of Theology and Ethics.

Russell Duke, Ph.D., is Associate Dean and Professor in the Azusa Pacific Graduate School of Theology. Dr. Duke also served as Interim Dean of the Graduate School of Theology.

Timothy Finlay, Ph.D., is Associate Professor of Old Testament in the Azusa Pacific Graduate School of Theology.

Deborah Hearn-Chung Gin, Ph.D., is Associate Professor of Ministry in the Azusa Pacific Graduate School of Theology, and Faculty Fellow in the Center for Teaching, Learning, and Assessment.

Lynn Allan Losie, Ph.D., is Associate Professor of New Testament in the Azusa Pacific Graduate School of Theology. Dr. Losie also served as Chair of the Department of Biblical Studies.

Brian Lugioyo, Ph.D., is Associate Professor of Theology and Ethics in the Azusa Pacific Graduate School of Theology, and Director of the Kern Scholars Program.

Kevin W. Mannoia, Ph.D., is Chaplain for Faculty, Staff, and Graduate Students at Azusa Pacific University. Dr. Mannoia also served as Dean of the Azusa Pacific Graduate School of Theology.

Keith Matthews, D.Min., is Professor of Spiritual Formation and Contemporary Culture in the Azusa Pacific Graduate School of Theology, and Chair of the Department of Ministry. Dr. Matthews also served as Interim Director of the Doctor of Ministry Program.

Rob Muthiah, Ph.D., is Professor of Practical Theology in the Azusa Pacific Graduate School of Theology, and Director of Field Education. Dr. Muthiah also served as Director of the Kern Scholars Program.

Daniel Newman, Ph.D., is Professor of Practical Theology in the Azusa Pacific Graduate School of Theology, and Director of the Doctor of Ministry Korean Program in Los Angeles. Dr. Newman also served as Director of the Masters Korean Program in Los Angeles.

Linda Pyun, Ph.D., is Associate Professor of Christian Education in the Azusa Pacific Graduate School of Theology, and Director of the Masters Korean Program in Los Angeles.

Sarah Sumner, Ph.D., was Professor of Theology and Ministry at the Azusa Pacific Graduate School of Theology. Dr. Sumner also served as Chair of the Department of Ministry, and Special Assistant to the Dean.

Don Thorsen, Ph.D., is Professor of Theology in the Azusa Pacific Graduate School of Theology, and Chair of the Department of Theology and Ethics. Dr. Thorsen also served as Chair of the Department of Advanced Studies.

Kent Walkemeyer, D.Min., is Associate Professor of Ministry in the Azusa Pacific Graduate School of Theology, and Director of the Friends Center.

Roger White, Ed.D., is Professor of Educational Ministries in the Ministry Department of Azusa Pacific Graduate School of Theology, and Curator of Special Collections and Rare Books in the University Libraries. Dr. White also served as Interim Director of the Doctor of Ministry Program.

Karen Strand Winslow, Ph.D., is Professor of Biblical Studies in the Azusa Pacific Graduate School of Theology and Chair of the Department of Biblical Studies. Dr. Winslow also served as Director of the Free Methodist Center.

www.ingramcontent.com/pod-product-compliance
Lightning Source LLC
Chambersburg PA
CBHW021141230426
43667CB00005B/215